SATAN'S *Dirty Little* SECRET

THE TWO DEMON SPIRITS THAT ALL DEMONS GET THEIR STRENGTH FROM

STEVE FOSS

CHARISMA
HOUSE

SATAN'S DIRTY LITTLE SECRET by Steve Foss
Published by Charisma House
Charisma Media/Charisma House Book Group
600 Rinehart Road
Lake Mary, Florida 32746
www.charismahouse.com

Cover design by Bill Johnson

Visit the author's website at www.stevefoss.com.

Library of Congress Cataloging-in-Publication Data:

Foss, Steve.
  Satan's dirty little secret / Steve Foss.
      p. cm.
  Includes bibliographical references (p.   ).
  ISBN 978-1-61638-650-4 (trade paper) -- ISBN
978-1-61638-709-9 (ebook) 1. Spiritual warfare. 2.
Temptation. 3. Devil. 4. Demonology. I. Title.
  BV4509.5.F63 2012
  241'.3--dc23

                                        2011039350

While the author has made every effort to provide
accurate Internet addresses at the time of publication,
neither the publisher nor the author assumes any
responsibility for errors or for changes that occur after
publication.

Portions of this book were previously published
by Creation House, copyright © 2007, ISBN
978-1-59979-204-0.

12 13 14 15 16 — 9 8 7 6 5 4 3 2 1
Printed in the United States of America

CONTENTS

FOREWORD

GOD HAS TRULY used Pastor Steve Foss to expose some of the most pernicious strategies used by the devil to sideline God's people from fulfilling their potential. Steve's revelations do not come from an ivory tower but from face-to-face ministry with tens of thousands of young people and hundreds of thousands on the foreign field and in revival services all over America.

Through Steve's diligence in applying what I taught him—not to deal with the surface issues but to go into the spirit world to defeat the enemy—Steve has been rewarded with valuable nuggets of truth to share with the body of Christ on the devil's devices.

—DR. MORRIS CERULLO
PRESIDENT, MORRIS CERULLO WORLD EVANGELISM

INTRODUCTION

THERE ARE TIMES and seasons when God has opened the eyes of a generation into the spirit realm and revealed hidden truths. We are living in one of those seasons. The spirit of wisdom and revelation has been opening the eyes of God's people like never before. The strategies of Satan are being unmasked, and the church is about to embark on the greatest season of warfare and victory that it has ever known.

The prophetic nature of this book may make it a bit difficult to digest. The exposing of hidden strongholds is never an easy thing to experience. We all like to feel we are doing pretty well, but God wants us to be free. Scripture declares that he whom the Son sets free is free indeed (John 8:36). Only as we come into truth will we be free.

The truths discussed in this prophetic writing will challenge even the most committed Christian. It is hard-hitting at times and fast-paced. Take time to read and reread the chapters. Let the Spirit of God bring you into the depths of freedom that only come from deep calling unto deep (Ps. 42:7).

The purpose of this prophetic writing is not to entertain with cute stories and anecdotes. It's to break the back of the enemy's greatest hidden strategy and bring God's people to new levels of freedom. I pray that the anointing of God will be upon you and that the words of Christ will change you.

1

SATAN'S STRATEGY EXPOSED

For we are not ignorant of [Satan's] devices.
—2 CORINTHIANS 2:11

F OR WE ARE not ignorant of [Satan's] devices" (2 Cor. 2:11, KJV). This was the declaration the apostle Paul made two thousand years ago—a declaration of an awareness of the strategies of the enemy, an awareness that has been lost in our day. The traps that the enemy has set for us today are the same as they were two thousand years ago. Satan is doing nothing new today. He has not yet had an original idea. He is playing the same game he played in the Garden of Eden.

If you're like many Christians, you've probably thought that if you had been in that garden, you surely wouldn't have disobeyed God's command and eaten of the tree of the knowledge of good and evil (Gen. 2:17). Yet every day of our lives we are presented with this same temptation. Satan challenges us with the same questions he posed to Eve. And, unfortunately, most days we eat of the tree. The fruit binds us, holds us, and dictates almost every move we make.

The war to overcome sin often seems to be an overwhelming task for most. We believe in the finished work of Jesus on the cross, and yet we are bound by this continual cycle of yielding to temptation. Some of you reading this may be feeling a bit smug right now because you think you have a good handle on sin. You may be in a worse condition. The reality is that the church tends to limit sin to the major moral sins—lying,

1

cheating, adultery, fornication, drunkenness, and such like. Yet the stronghold of sin goes so much deeper in our lives.

Sin affects how we think, what we imagine, what we buy, sell, gather, and give. It affects how we worship, work, and live every aspect of our lives. It leads us into wrong relationships and to wrongly relate to one another. Sin dominates our viewpoints, our work ethics, and, most disturbingly, it dominates how we conduct ministry.

The same fruit from that same tree in the garden is being offered to all of us throughout our lives, and we keep eating it, often in the name of God. The focal point of all of our troubles is the tree of the knowledge of good and evil. This is where it all begins and where it can end. It is what happens here on a daily basis that will determine if the victory Christ has purchased for us will become a living reality in our lives. Once again God is about to open the eyes of a generation to the strategies of Satan.

By revelation God is going to destroy Satan's most powerful advantage: his ability to operate in the midst of ignorance. In this book we are going to uncover Satan's most diabolic strategy—how it works and how it affects our lives. We are going to expose his devices and start down the path of true freedom. I pray that together we will have an Isaiah experience and say, "Woe is me! for I am undone" (Isa. 6:5, kjv). Oh, that God would give us such an encounter with truth that the strongholds of the tree of the knowledge of good and evil are permanently broken in our lives.

The Vision

It was early 1991. I was the youth pastor at a church in Georgia. I had only been on the job for two months when I was invited to speak at the local high school's Christian Bible study. They asked if I would speak two weeks in a row. I readily accepted and began to plan my strategy.

You see, this was hard-core Baptist country—Southern Baptist, conservative, don't-give-me-that-Pentecostal-stuff country. I, on the other hand, was a hard-core Holy Ghost–filled, tongues-talking, hands-laying, miracle-believing, prophecy-preaching fireball. I knew that this Bible study had about seventy in attendance every Wednesday morning. I also knew that all except a handful of them came from noncharismatic/Pentecostal backgrounds.

They gave me about fifteen minutes to speak. My strategy was this. I would preach a basic word on the revelation of Jesus the first week, then hit them with the power of God the second week. The first week went exactly as I had planned. I preached, and they were quite engaged. The revelation anointing flowed strong. By the end of the fifteen minutes they were on the edge of their seats wanting more. I had them right where I wanted them. The next week I was going to blast them.

The day before the second meeting I shut myself off for an extended time of prayer. I knew that if I was going to see the power of God break out on this campus, I was going to have to fight some intensive spiritual warfare. I had been trained by my spiritual father, Dr. Morris Cerullo, in how to tear down demonic strongholds over a region. As I went to prayer I had no idea that what was about to transpire was going to forever change the course of my life.

During that time of prayer I had two visions. The first vision was of the upcoming meeting itself. I saw a young man whom I had never met. I saw myself calling him to come and stand up front. I then prophesied over him about the call of God on his life. Then I simply spoke the word of the Lord over him, and he fell under the power of the Spirit. In the vision I saw his face and exactly where he would be sitting.

When I stood up to speak the next day at the meeting, there he was. And he was sitting exactly where I had seen him in the vision. I preached for a few minutes on experiencing the power of God. Then I called this young man out. He came and stood before me. He was from a non-Spirit-filled background and had no idea what was about to transpire.

I had no helpers with me, so I asked for somebody to come and stand behind him. The volunteer didn't know what was going to happen. I then proceeded to prophesy over this young man about the call of God on his life to preach. He began to weep. He said that the previous night he told his mother for the first time that he felt God was calling him to be a preacher.

I then looked him in the eyes, standing five feet away from him, and said, "Jesus fill him with Your power right now!" As soon as I spoke, a wave of God's power swept through that room and hit this young man. He immediately flew backward under God's power. He landed in the arms of the volunteer, who was in total shock. I turned just in time to see seventy mouths drop open and all heads turn as this young man was being blasted by the power of God. It was all I could do to keep from laughing when I saw the sheer look of shock on their faces.

All together they looked at the young man, then looked at me, and then back at the young man. You could hear gasps all over the room. I opened the Word to share a couple of scriptures on what just happened. Then the bell rang, and they slowly, in shock, filed out of the room. Needless to say, I was the talk of the school by the end of the day.

Much transpired at that school over the next several months, but that will have to wait for another book. As awesome as this was, it was the second vision that changed my life. After I had this first vision about the young man, I began to go into spiritual warfare prayer. I began to bind specific demon spirits, the ones you would expect to be operating at a high school. I bound lust, drugs, hate, unforgiveness, fornication, pornography, violence, drunkenness, and such like.

I had a fair amount of experience in spiritual warfare and

had gained a great sense of what was going on in the spirit realm. I could sense whether the stronghold was breaking and when it broke. This day, however, it felt like I couldn't make any headway. I prayed and prayed, but each of these spirits seemed to not be moved.

As I pressed deeper into prayer, I had an open vision. I saw the entire school as if I was standing several hundred yards away. I saw the ground, the campus, the sky, and something very strange.

I saw coming out from under the ground two giant tentacles, one from the left of the campus and the other from the right. They were very thick near the ground and got thinner as they rose higher. The two tentacles interlaced themselves as they met over the top of the center of the campus. They gripped each other powerfully. They were huge.

Then I noticed that attached all along these two tentacles were demon spirits. Each had a name written on it: lust, hate, drunkenness, and so forth. They each had what looked like two arms with which they grabbed hold of the tentacles. They didn't hold them on the outside. They were actually rooted into the tentacles themselves.

When I saw them, I began to bind them in Jesus's name. I called out lust by name and commanded it to go. I saw this demon of lust get powerfully buffeted and blown backward. It was like a leaf during a strong gust of wind. It bowed back and shook, but its roots in the tentacles were undamaged. I went from demon to demon, and the same thing happened. The more I prayed, the harder they got hit. I started to realize that if they didn't have roots in the two tentacles, my prayers would have easily driven them away from the campus and the students.

As this vision continued, I asked the Lord, "What are these two tentacles?" I knew if I could break their power, all the others would easily go. The Lord spoke to me these words that have changed my life. God said, "These are the two demon spirits that all other spirits get their strength from."

These two demon spirits empower all the other demon spirits. This was the mother lode of revelation. God then said, "They are the same two spirits that Satan released upon Eve in the garden. They are the same two demon spirits that Satan continues to release today."

I cried out to God, "What are they? What are their names?" I could easily see the names of all the smaller demons, but I couldn't see any names on these. It amazed me how the demons we all think are so big and powerful were actually quite small. Lust, drunkenness, drug addiction, violence, hatred, and fear were all small and relatively weak without these two giant demon spirits.

I prayed for quite a while. I knew I had to go deep in the spirit to see what was under the surface. After quite a while the vision expanded. Now not only could I see above the ground, but I also saw under the ground below the campus. Each of the tentacles curved back toward each other and nearly touched. They looked like giant roots—like a bulb, fat at the bottom and thinner as it got farther away from the root.

Written on these roots were their names. One was called *insecurity*, and the other was called *inferiority*.

2

A SETUP IN THE GARDEN

Then the serpent said to the woman, "You will not surely die. For God knows that in the day you eat of it your eyes will be opened, and you will be like God, knowing good and evil."

—GENESIS 3:4–5

WHEN GOD SHOWED me the names of these two demon spirits, I didn't fully understand. I didn't even really understand what inferiority meant. So I grabbed a dictionary to look up these two words. The word *insecurity* means "the state of being not secure, not confident, not firm."[1] The word *inferiority* means "the state of feeling lower in position, stature, or value."[2] God spoke to me during the vision that these are the same two demon spirits that Satan released upon Eve in the garden. So after looking up the definitions, I went to Genesis:

> Now the serpent was more subtil than any beast of the field which the LORD God had made. And he said unto the woman, Yea, hath God said, Ye shall not eat of every tree of the garden? And the woman said unto the serpent, We may eat of the fruit of the trees of the garden: but of the fruit of the tree which is in the midst of the garden, God hath said, Ye shall not eat of it, neither shall ye touch it, lest ye die. And the serpent said unto the woman, Ye shall not surely die: for God doth know

that in the day ye eat thereof, then your eyes shall be opened, and ye shall be as gods, knowing good and evil. And when the woman saw that the tree was good for food, and that it was pleasant to the eyes, and a tree to be desired to make one wise, she took of the fruit thereof, and did eat, and gave also unto her husband with her; and he did eat.

—Genesis 3:1–6, kjv

"Yea, hath God said, Ye shall not eat of every tree of the garden?" Thus the setup begins. Satan's very first step was to call into question the Word of God. Everything Adam and Eve knew to be true was based solely on what God had spoken to them. God's Word was their only source of truth. They walked with God and talked with God. He gave them the commands concerning the garden and the tree of the knowledge of good and evil.

All of Eve's security was based on the assumption that everything God said was true. God spoke it, and that settled it. She had never even considered questioning the truthfulness of God's Word. Satan's strategy was to set her up so he could call into question the truthfulness of God's Word. So he presented a question in which he misquoted what God had said. Satan said, "Yea, hath God said, Ye shall not eat of every tree of the garden?" (Gen. 3:1, kjv). Eve promptly responded with what God had actually said: "And the woman said unto the serpent, We may eat of the fruit of the trees of the garden: But of the fruit of the tree which is in the midst of the garden, God hath said, Ye shall not eat of it, neither shall ye touch it, lest ye die" (Gen. 3:2–3, kjv).

Eve at this point correctly responded to the false statement. But she was now engaged in a conversation in which she shouldn't have engaged. Satan was now ready to release the first of the two demon spirits upon Eve. "And the serpent said unto the woman, Ye shall not surely die" (Gen. 3:4, kjv).

The first demon spirit was now released. He released upon her *insecurity*.

He knew that her whole security was based upon her absolute trust that everything God said was true. Now all of a sudden she is confronted with the possibility that God was a liar. She began to feel that her whole world was collapsing around her. She felt that she could no longer trust in the sure Word of God. She began to feel *insecure*.

Without hesitation Satan released the second of this dynamic duo of demon spirits, *inferiority*. He said, "For God doth know that in the day ye eat thereof, then your eyes shall be opened, and ye shall be as gods, knowing good and evil" (Gen. 3:5, KJV). Now, not only is she being assaulted by insecurity, feeling like everything she knew to be true is being called into question, but Eve believes she is not who she thought she was.

THE IMAGE OF GOD

The Bible declares in Genesis 1:27, "So God created man in His own image; in the image of God He created him; male and female He created them." Adam and Eve were already in the image of God. They were of full spiritual stature. God never intended for man to have the knowledge of good and evil. Satan took what was good and made it sound bad. Eve now felt that she had been held out on—that she was lacking something. She felt less in position or stature. She now felt *inferior*.

Satan had her right where he wanted her. She felt insecure and inferior. Flooded with these new emotions, she was now overwhelmed and desperate to regain her sense of security and stature. At this point, although her emotions were overwhelming her, she hadn't actually lost either her real security or her stature. She only now believed she had.

With these emotions running high and these two demon spirits assaulting Eve, Satan then gave her the knockout punch. He offered her a solution to her dilemma in the midst of the attack. He said, "*Then your eyes shall be opened, and ye shall be as gods*, knowing good and evil" (Gen. 3:5, KJV, emphasis added). "Eve, all you have to do is eat of this fruit, and you will have your security back and you will have your position back. 'Ye shall be as gods.'"

She reached out and grabbed the fruit. When she bit into it, in disobedience to God's Word, she lost the very thing she was trying to regain. She now lost her security and her stature. She was now fallen. Satan had succeeded. Man had sinned against God, and the pure union between God and man was broken. Death now entered into mankind: spiritual death, emotional death, relational death, and ultimately physical death.

The partaking of the fruit caused the very thing from which Eve was trying to get free. From this point on man would forever fight this same battle. Insecurity and inferiority had now entered into the world, and all the other demon spirits had their access point upon which to attack and enslave mankind. Satan has not changed his strategy. Still to this day he uses the same two demon spirits to open mankind to partake of the deadly fruit that enslaves.

3

THE SIN OF COMPARISON

But they measuring themselves by themselves, and com-
paring themselves among themselves, are not wise.
—2 Corinthians 10:12, KJV

I NSECURITY AND INFERIORITY are the doorways through which every other spirit gains entrance. In the garden Eve was deceived into believing God had lied to her and that she wasn't who she thought she was. She felt insecure because she didn't know what the truth was. She felt inferior because she thought God had misled her and was actually withholding His best. To this day the same two lies permeate our society. There has been an unending assault on the validity of God's Word. Everywhere you turn, the challenge to God's Word is evident.

Simply turn on the evening news or a sitcom and you will hear the questioning of God's Word and principles. People call evil good and good evil. Constantly the values, truths, and authority of the Word of God are challenged and called into question.

Even in churches across America preachers are afraid to preach the unadulterated Word of God. They preach a God of love but avoid the God of judgment. Isn't it interesting that the serpent also avoided the subject of judgment? He said that God will not judge you. "Ye shall not surely die" (Gen. 3:4, KJV).

We preach a culturally sensitive gospel that often is not God-sensitive. We are more interested in attracting people with a positive message than bringing to them the only thing that can make them free. Eve's only ability to resist the ploys of the enemy was to rely on the truth of God's Word. Before we go deeper into the revelation of insecurity and inferiority and how it affects almost every part of our lives, we need to look back at the original sin.

Original Sin

Lucifer was the highest of all angels. His beauty was beyond all. There was no one greater than him except God:

> You were the anointed cherub who covers; I established you; you were on the holy mountain of God; you walked back and forth in the midst of fiery stones. You were perfect in your ways from the day you were created.
> —Ezekiel 28:14–15

In this state of absolute perfection a most horrific event took place: Lucifer got his eyes off of God and onto himself.

> Thine heart was lifted up because of *thy beauty*, thou hast corrupted thy wisdom by reason of *thy brightness*: I will cast thee to the ground, I will lay thee before kings, that they may behold thee.
> —Ezekiel 28:17, kjv, emphasis added

The Scripture declares that iniquity first happened *in* him—in his heart.

> Thou wast perfect in thy ways from the day that thou wast created, *till iniquity was found in thee.*
> —Ezekiel 28:15, kjv, emphasis added

Lucifer began to compare himself with God and with others. With God, he saw that God's beauty surpassed his own. With creation, he realized his beauty and brightness were unmatched. He felt inferior to God and superior to others. His solution was simple.

> For thou hast said in thine heart, I will ascend into heaven, I will exalt my throne above the stars of God: I will sit also upon the mount of the congregation, in the sides of the north: I will ascend above the heights of the clouds; *I will be like the most High.*
>
> —Isaiah 14:13–14, kjv, emphasis added

He compared himself with another. He wanted to make himself like God. In order for inferiority to exist, there must be a comparison. Suppose a child is born in a remote village and has never had contact with any other people outside of his village. Let's also suppose that everyone in his village has really large ears. Although he sees the large ears, it seems normal to him. But let him get introduced to a village where the people have small ears, and he will immediately begin to compare. He will look at them and notice the difference. Most often he will then either feel inferior or superior to these people.

He has engaged in what I call the sin of comparison. You look to yourself, and then compare yourself with another. This is what Lucifer did in heaven. It is what the serpent had Eve do in the garden:

> For God [Elohiym] doth know that in the day ye eat thereof, then your eyes shall be opened, and ye *shall be as gods* [elohiym], knowing good and evil.
>
> —Genesis 3:5, kjv, emphasis added

It is the same thing we all do every day of our lives. We are constantly comparing ourselves in all sorts of situations. Stop for a moment and think through the last few hours of your day. How often have you thought this person or that person was smart or dumb, beautiful or homely, nice or mean, rude or kind, arrogant or humble?

We are constantly comparing ourselves to others and others to ourselves. We, as Christians, also do this. We are always measuring ourselves by ourselves. We wish we were more spiritual like so-and-so or that we had a bigger church like the one down the street. Or we take the other side of the coin on our "successes" and feel we are better than others because of those accomplishments. The Bible calls comparison a sin. When we measure ourselves by ourselves, we are not being wise.

> For we dare not make ourselves of the number, or compare ourselves with some that commend themselves: but they *measuring themselves by themselves*, and comparing themselves among themselves, *are not wise.*
> —2 Corinthians 10:12, kjv, emphasis added

God doesn't want us to compare ourselves with one another. He says this is not wise. In order to enter into comparison, we have to be inwardly oriented. We have to be looking to ourselves first. When we head down this path of comparison, we end up making a judgment about who we are—about our current state.

> But with me it is a very small thing that I should be judged by you or by a human court. In fact, *I do not even judge myself.* For I know nothing against myself, yet I am not justified by this; but *He who judges me is the Lord.*
> —1 Corinthians 4:3–4, emphasis added

Paul realized that he didn't have a true perspective of himself. Even if he thought he was innocent in all areas, he realized that he couldn't have a true understanding outside of God. When we begin down the path of comparison, we have entered the pathway of deception. We begin to judge by our own perspectives, views, opinions, likes, and dislikes. It leads us to not have our eyes on God; thus we don't see truth.

In every aspect of life we compare things. Something is hot, or something is cold. This is not what I am referring to here. It is when the comparisons cause us to make judgments about ourselves toward others that we have started down this slippery slope.

Comparison is the first step toward insecurity and inferiority. Once insecurity and inferiority take root, they give every other demon spirit a foothold upon which to attach themselves. The problem always starts when we get our eyes off God.

4

THE ADVERTISING TRAP

*I am crucified with Christ: nevertheless I live; yet not I, but Christ
liveth in me: and the life which I now live in the flesh I live by the
faith of the Son of God, who loved me, and gave himself for me.*
—GALATIANS 2:20, KJV

TODAY WE ARE inundated with an unprecedented number
of messages and images all vying for our attention.
Never before in human history has mankind had to deal
with such a continual flood tide of information. In just one day
of watching television you can be filled with more new information and images than an old-world person may have received
in a lifetime.

Everyone is trying to get their message across to us in order
to persuade us to their way of thinking. This is no more evident
than in the arena of advertising. Advertising has been refined
to an art that has the ability to cause the masses to reach out
and buy a product, even when the product isn't that good.

In the movie industry the studios have learned how to,
with a slick ad campaign, pull in large crowds to the opening
weekend of a relatively lame movie. In the consumer product
industry, advertisers have utilized one of Satan's strategies
in order to seduce society into buying their wares. Without
demonizing consumerism, we must take an honest look at our
capitalistic society and the inroads the enemy has made into it.
If we don't begin to recognize Satan's strategies, we will constantly be swayed by them and brought into levels of bondage.

We must first recognize that the American economy is not driven by biblical principles for the purpose of advancing the kingdom of heaven. The American capitalistic system is driven predominately by greed. When we hear revelations of corporations "cooking the books" to inflate their companies' value in order for a few to steal millions of dollars, we are seeing evidence of this greed.

We should not be shocked by these kinds of revelations. Much more than this has been going on, but most of the perpetrators are never caught. Most companies are motivated to make money at any cost. They are not interested in your personal well-being, except where that interest means a potential increase in profits.

Once again I must stress that I am not trying to demonize all businesses. There are many godly people in business who operate under a higher calling than simply a mission to make money. If it weren't for these godly people in our society, things would be much worse. Yet even with these people, much of our Western culture is still driven by greed.

In the consumer product industry we find the use of insecurity and inferiority in advertisement prevalent. They are used to make you want to buy a product in order to alleviate your insecurity or inferiority. For example, in the early 1970s people didn't really have a problem with a person who had an occasional itch on the head. Then a company began to run a successful ad campaign showing a handsome man and beautiful woman on a crash course to a romantic meeting. Then suddenly one of them would scratch an itch on his head, and the other would be disgusted and totally put off by this.

The message being sent was obvious: people will think less of you if you have dandruff (inferiority). Then the commercial would show the same person in the shower using a certain shampoo. In the final scene, the same two people on another crash course for a romantic meeting. But this time, because the shampoo was used, there was no embarrassing itchy, flaky scalp. They met, and it was love at first sight.

This advertisement played right into the enemy's plan to unleash the spirits of insecurity and inferiority upon society. The commercials basically said, "If you don't buy this product, you will miss out on the love of your life. You will be a less attractive person. So, here, take this and eat of it. It will make you wise, strong, powerful, and influential." Sound familiar?

Many companies use this same strategy. Car companies are notorious for this. If you drive such-and-such car, then you will have the respect of others. Beautiful people will be drawn to you. It will be a status symbol. You are superior with it and inferior without it.

Fashion rides on this principle too. God forbid you get caught wearing last year's fashion. Why? Is it because the clothes are worn out? Not hardly. It's because the industry has done a masterful job of making us feel insecure and inferior if we don't have the newest, latest, best, and so on. This is how designer clothes can sell for so much. The advertising says you are better if you wear Tommy Hilfiger. You are cooler if you have Air Jordans. The list goes on and on.

Our society is obsessed with how we look. We spend billions of wasted dollars on apparel we rarely ever use. Closets are filled with last year's fashions, which won't be used again because we wouldn't be caught dead wearing them: shoes, coats, jackets, hats—you name it.

Insecurity and inferiority are, perhaps, no more prevalent than in the health and fitness industries. We are told through advertising and the media that hyper-thin is in. If you have a little padding on your midsection, then you are less attractive. And being less attractive makes you feel insecure and inferior.

Where did we ever get this perverse idea about our value? God clearly declared that true beauty is found within (1 Pet. 3:3–4). Yet we ignore His Word and are just as driven as the world to improve our appearance. We diet to no end. We join health clubs and spend billions on exercise machines—all just to get that "perfect" body.

Who wouldn't like to lose a little weight or trim and tone those flabby areas of our bodies? Who wouldn't want the six-pack abs we always see on TV and in magazines? There's nothing wrong with getting fit, but most of our modern exercise and diet craze isn't really about health but about personal appearance.

You may say, "Brother Steve, is it wrong to want to look good?" My response is simple. Look good in whose eyes? Whom are you trying to impress? Whose attention are you trying to get? What lack in yourself are you trying to fill? If insecurity and/or inferiority are at the root of your desire to improve your looks, then you are once again eating of the tree of the knowledge of good and evil. Once again you are feeding your insecurities and inferiorities.

Now, it is not wrong to diet or work out and exercise. These can be very good for you if they are done for the right reason. The reason must be to have a healthy body to better serve God with. When that is the true motivation for your fitness craze, you will never be concerned with the size of your biceps, how cut your abs are, or if you still have little areas with cellulite.

People get nose jobs, breast implants, and tummy tucks all to alleviate their insecurities and inferiorities. We are manipulated by the latest trends. In the 1970s it was sexy for a man to have a hairy chest. Now it's not, and many men shave their chests in order to have that *GQ* look.

When I was a young teen, if a guy wore an earring, he was gay. Then a homosexual musician, still in the closet, started wearing an earring in his left ear, claiming this was cool. So multitudes of young men started wearing earrings in their left ear because it was still a sign of being gay to wear one in the right ear or in both lobes. Today guys have earrings in both ears, their tongues, lips, belly buttons—everywhere. They think it makes them look cooler or even that it makes them superior.

From our hairstyles, clothes, and physical appearance to the products we buy and cars we drive, we are a people driven by our need to alleviate our sense of insecurity and inferiority. Advertisers tap into this need and exploit it for their personal gain. When your eyes are opened and you begin to see this, it can become a little overwhelming.

How, when we are surrounded by such an onslaught of temptation to feed our insecurities and inferiorities, do we ever walk free? In later chapters we will deal in-depth with God's solution, but this one verse really sums it up: "I am crucified with Christ: nevertheless I live; yet not I, but Christ liveth in me: and the life which I now live in the flesh I live by the faith of the Son of God, who loved me, and gave himself for me" (Gal. 2:20, KJV). The key to total victory is to stop living for ourselves and live for Him only.

5

THE MONEY PIT

No one can serve two masters; for either he will hate the one and love the other, or else he will be loyal to the one and despise the other. You cannot serve God and mammon.

—MATTHEW 6:24

THE WORKINGS OF insecurity and inferiority are clearly evident in the area of finances. For as long as history has been recorded, mankind has used a person's wealth to judge his value. We have, through the centuries, equated wealth with value. I was reminded of this again the other day. I was watching TV when the movie *Titanic* came on. As if I had never seen the movie before, I was horrified once again when the first-class passengers were given the limited lifeboat space while the poor passengers were locked in the decks below.

Our modern society thinks we have mostly overcome such blatant discrimination, but the truth is far worse than many want to admit. Much of the Western world is still driven by a desire to attain financial security and prosperity.

While on a ministry trip during the early 1990s, I preached at a friend's church in downtown Detroit. During my visit, I went for a walk with my pastor-friend, who lived in a low-income, mostly African American neighborhood. As we walked, I was shocked to see newer model Mercedes and BMWs in the driveways of these little run-down houses. I couldn't imagine how so many of the people managed to afford such expensive cars. So I asked my friend, and what he told me opened my eyes.

He said there were two things that were most important to the people he grew up around: the car they drove and the clothes they wore. He said some people would go hungry just so they could buy a designer shirt. They would go deep into debt just so they could have that BMW. He told me that having these things made them feel like they were somebody. (Inferiority rears its ugly head again!)

Instead of being content with what they had, they would put themselves in financial slavery simply to have the illusion of prosperity, because to them wealth equaled value and status. In their eyes it had the power to make them superior. This is not limited at all to any one ethnic group. It is the disease of our times—from kids killing other kids over a pair of designer running shoes to families going into bankruptcy in record numbers because they tried to keep up with the Joneses. The saying "keeping up with the Joneses" is all about feeding our insecurity and inferiority.

I grew up in a middle-class neighborhood and had the perfect *Leave It to Beaver* family, and the pressure to keep up with the Joneses was definitely alive and well in our community too. My mother used to tell me stories about what it was like for her when she was a young wife and mother. She said a woman's house and kitchen floors had to be perfect all the time, and she was always so embarrassed that her floors weren't as nice as the neighbors'. She'd wax and wax, but they never looked as good. Finally, she found out the secret. The other women had a professional service come in and clean their floors. So she had to have the professional service come to her house too. God forbid that her floors weren't as perfect as everyone else's!

We spend and borrow to gain a sense of security and value. This is why when people are under financial stress, they often pull out the credit cards and buy something. The illusion created when we swipe the plastic and don't actually have to pay for the item right then gives us a sense of power and control. It makes us feel we are wealthier than we are, which momentarily alleviates our sense of insecurity and inferiority.

Often we buy the biggest, most expensive house we can possibly get a loan for. If it weren't for the banks limiting us, many of us would try to get an even more expensive house. We end up with long-term mortgages well into our seventies when we should have owned our homes free and clear in order to pass them on to the next generation. We are so desperate to feel like we are succeeding financially that we are willing to mortgage not only our future but our children's as well.

Whom Will You Serve?

We do all of this in direct violation of the Word of God. We look to wealth and money to make us feel better about ourselves, but the apostle Paul gives us another way to live. He wrote in Philippians 4:11, "Not that I speak in regard to need, for I have learned in whatever state I am, to be content." We go into debt to feed our desires or our families' lusts, but the Scriptures say, "Owe no one anything except to love one another" (Rom. 13:8).

I am not saying that God doesn't want us to have nice things, but we should ask ourselves why we want them. Is it to feed some deep sense of insecurity and inferiority? So often it is. God says for us to be content with what we have (Heb. 13:5), but many of us want so much more—the newest car, latest gadget, trendiest fashion, finest house, and on and on. Instead we should seek first the kingdom of God and His righteousness, and all these things will be added to us (Matt. 6:33).

Being concerned about acquiring things can be one of your greatest enemies in life because it can keep us from bearing fruit. Matthew 13:22 says, "Now he who received seed among the thorns is he who hears the word, and the *cares of this world* and the *deceitfulness of riches* choke the word, and *he becomes unfruitful*" (emphasis added). Why does he become unfruitful? For two reasons:

1. "The cares of this world," meaning the distractions of this present age

2. "The deceitfulness of riches," meaning the delusion that wealth and possessions provide worth and safety

These two things will choke out the Word of God—make it fruitless in our lives. This battle is one of our most challenging because so many of us have believed a lie that wealth and possessions bring value and security. We keep eating the fruit of wealth, or the illusion of wealth, to give our lives value. When we do this, we have bowed down to the god of mammon, and those of us in the church are not immune to this idolatry.

One of the great dangers of this is that those who are in the church can use the promises of God to serve their lust for things. They actually try to make God their servant in order to get what they really feel they need—wealth. God warns us of this: "No one can serve two masters; for either he will hate the one and love the other, or else he will be loyal to the one and despise the other. You cannot serve God and mammon" (Matt. 6:24).

In life you will serve either God or mammon. The other will be your servant. Many who think they are serving God are actually serving mammon because they look to it as their source. How many times have we said, "All I need is some more money, and I can do this or that?" So often we have looked to money and wealth as the "answer" to our problems.

Let me be clear: I believe in biblical prosperity. I teach it with boldness. However, just as it is counterproductive to preach deliverance to an alcoholic while giving him a drink, so is it futile to preach prosperity to those who serve mammon.

Those who look to money to give them a sense of value and security will misuse the truth of biblical prosperity to feed their insecurities and inferiorities.

You can hardly turn on the TV without seeing an infomercial advertising some new business opportunity that will provide two things: security and the good life—in other words, value. We buy the programs, join the clubs, and attend the meetings all in the hope of attaining financial security and freedom. We as Christians tell ourselves we will be able to help so many other people once we get the money from this program or that business. But for most of us, somewhere deep at the root of this desire to attain wealth is a devastating lie: money is the answer.

God can provide all you and I need without money. He may, and often does, use money to take care of us, but He alone is our answer. He is our source. That is what Jesus was addressing in Matthew 6:24 when He said no one can love God and mammon. The next several verses point to the true source of our security.

> Therefore I say to you, do not worry about your life, what you will eat or what you will drink; nor about your body, what you will put on. Is not life more than food and the body more than clothing? Look at the birds of the air, for they neither sow nor reap nor gather into barns; yet your heavenly Father feeds them. Are you not of more value than they? Which of you by worrying can add one cubit to his stature?
>
> So why do you worry about clothing? Consider the lilies of the field, how they grow: they neither toil nor spin; and yet I say to you that even Solomon in all his glory was not arrayed like one of these. Now if God so clothes the grass of the field, which today is, and tomorrow is thrown into the oven,

will He not much more clothe you, O you of little
faith? Therefore do not worry, saying, "What shall
we eat?" or "What shall we drink?" or "What shall
we wear?" *For after all these things the Gentiles seek.*
For your heavenly Father knows that you need all
these things. *But seek first the kingdom* of God and
His righteousness, and *all these things shall be added
to you.* Therefore do not worry about tomorrow.
—MATTHEW 6:25–34, EMPHASIS ADDED

If we are looking to money as our answer, we have fallen
into the trap of the tree. We have believed the lie that God is
not sufficient, that He alone cannot sustain us. Philippians 4:19
assures us, "And my God shall supply all your need according
to His riches in glory by Christ Jesus." When he wrote that
letter to the Philippians, the apostle Paul had come to the
true understanding that God was his source, not wealth. So
if he had money, he was content. And if he didn't, he was still
content because he knew God would supply all his needs.

God is our source; money is our servant. The deception
that we can gain security and value from wealth wages a fierce
battle for our hearts and minds. This is why Jesus said, "It is
easier for a camel to go through the eye of a needle than for
a rich man to enter the kingdom of God" (Matt. 19:24). Jesus
didn't say this because money is evil. Jesus never had a problem
with people having wealth. He simply understood how wealth
feeds any insecurity and feeling of inferiority.

Jesus knew the trap the enemy set. He knew that many
people would not be able to look to God as their source because
they would believe the deception that wealth provides security
and value. This is why the rich young ruler went away sad in
Matthew 19 after Jesus told him, "If you want to be perfect, go,
sell what you have and give to the poor, and you will have treasure in heaven; and come, follow Me" (v. 21).

The rich young ruler put his trust in wealth, not God. Jesus gave him an opportunity to be delivered, but instead he walked away from Christ and embraced his riches (v. 22). Jesus wasn't glorifying poverty. He often spoke of the promise of abundance and blessings for those who would fully obey God. What He was addressing in Matthew 19 was the fruit of the tree of the knowledge of good and evil at work in the rich young ruler's life. I believe one of the reasons God sometimes challenges us to give a sacrificial offering is so we will remember that He is the source of our provision, not our checking account.

Don't be deceived by this trick of the enemy. Ask God to search your heart. Ask Him to expose the secret trust you may have put in money and wealth so the stronghold of the tree that exists through money and wealth can be broken over your life.

6

MISPLACED IDENTITY

You shall have no other gods before Me.... For I, the
LORD your God, am a jealous God.
—EXODUS 20:3–5

THE WORKINGS OF insecurity and inferiority are apparent in every area of life, including the church. When believers separate from one another because of doctrinal disputes, insecurity and inferiority are usually at the root.

Now, I firmly believe doctrine is important, and there are some doctrines that, if not held in proper order, can lead to much confusion and damage in the body of Christ. Yet very few are significant enough to cause Christians to isolate themselves and separate from one another. Only teachings that are truly doctrines of demons—which deny the deity of Christ and the completeness of His blood sacrifice to provide salvation for all who make Him Lord—should ever cause us to separate from one another. Most of the other disputes that cause churches to split should never produce isolation and separation. But they do—because of insecurity and inferiority.

Most people don't own their doctrines but are owned by them. What I mean is this: they actually gain their sense of identity from the doctrines themselves. The doctrines become who they are. You've no doubt heard people say, "I am a Calvinist" or "I am a Pentecostal" or "I am a Fundamentalist." These labels in and of themselves aren't bad. There's nothing wrong with using them to describe the form of Christian practice we follow. However, these labels become much more than that. They become our identity.

We gain a sense of security and belonging when we align with those who are like-minded. We gain a sense of value from our belief system and doctrine. We actually begin to feel a bit better about ourselves because we think we have been enlightened more than someone else. It gives us a sense of power and superiority. This way of thinking could escalate to a haughty spirit, but more often it is much subtler than that.

It is often just a feeling of being better because you're right. We all like being right. We all like being ahead of the rest, even just a little bit. We like having the sense of power and control that come from having a special insight into truth. It increases our personal sense of worth, and we begin to gain our identity from it. What we don't usually realize is that once we've crossed the deadly bridge of gaining our identity from doctrine, we have been snared by the trap of the tree.

Whatever you gain your identity from you will defend, protect, and promote! Once you gain your identity from something, it then owns you. If you gain your identity from doctrine, then doctrine owns you. You will defend, protect, and promote it, because in so doing, you are defending, protecting, and promoting yourself, your value, and your sense of worth.

We have all seen this at work in our churches. Somebody believes he has come into a new revelation. He hears a sermon or reads a book, and what he learns touches him on some deep emotional level. So he embraces the teaching and gains a new feeling of value.

Then he begins to promote the doctrine to others and is surprised that not everyone sees it the way he does. When his brothers and sisters in Christ challenge this new doctrine, the person becomes defensive and upset. Then he begins to fight to protect and defend the belief, which leads to strife. Often the person who embraced the new doctrine begins to line up with the accuser of the brethren and starts to attack his brothers and sisters by saying they are religious or deceived.

This attack is a defensive mechanism. The person isn't really interested in revealing truth. He is antagonistic toward his fellow believers because he needs to protect his newfound identity. It is all about self-preservation.

Often the individual will work to gather a small group who also believes this new doctrine. The group meets together informally and talks about how the pastor needs to be delivered or needs a new revelation. Even if the band of Christians is correct, they enter into covenant with a seditious spirit when they begin to isolate themselves from those who don't share their point of view.

Instead of embracing humility because of their new revelation, they begin to lay the groundwork for a coup. If they can't manipulate the existing church to go their way, they will feel "led by the Lord" to leave. A church disagreement has become a full-grown split, and the group has isolated themselves from others in the body.

The spirit of pride is working mightily among this group of believers as they pat themselves on the back for becoming free from that formerly oppressive, religious church. They now "have the truth" and will build God's kingdom "the way God wanted it to be done." They have no idea, but Satan is rejoicing. Once again the spirits of insecurity and inferiority have done their job and have led people to eat from the tree of the knowledge of good and evil. Man has again become bound, and the fruit of the enemy is spreading.

Even if the doctrine these people have embraced is correct, it is still wrong of them to allow it to own them. When they found their identity in their doctrine instead of Jesus, they fell into Satan's trap. God may have been trying to restore a truth, but evil polluted it instead.

Wanting to Fit In

People look to all kinds of things to give them a sense of identity, not only doctrine. Recently I was at a youth camp, and a teenage girl asked me if there was anything wrong with getting a tattoo. I knew she really didn't want an answer, just a justification for an act she had already determined in her heart to do. I still decided to respond to her by leading her to some principles. I said, "In the Old Testament…" As soon as I said that, she cut me off and said, "That's the Law. We're not under the Law."

I responded, "That is your wrong and ignorant thinking talking. Jesus didn't come to do away with the Law. He came to fulfill it. Murder is still sin. What you don't understand is that in the Law are principles. Those spiritual laws are still in effect today."

I continued, "Even the sanitation laws, like going so many paces outside your tent to dig a hole to go to the bathroom, still have underlying principles that if violated today will bring a form of judgment. The sanitation laws were given because man had no understanding of germs and microorganisms. If you go to the bathroom even now and don't wash your hands, or allow the toilet to overflow and not be cleaned, germs and disease will spread.

"The specific regulation may no longer be required, but the underlying truth that God was getting at still does. The same goes for the principle found in the Word about taking on the markings of the heathen nations."

I told her about Leviticus 19:28, which says, "You shall not make any cuttings in your flesh for the dead, nor tattoo any marks on you: I am the Lord." I continued to explain that the principle behind that particular law was that God's people are not to take on the identifying marks of groups that are enemies of God. I said to her, "What would you think of me if I showed up to preach wearing a satanic pentagram and some inverted crosses? Would you have a problem with me?"

She said, "Yes." Then I immediately responded, "How dare you judge me! You don't know my heart." She looked shocked. I concluded by saying, "Of course you know my heart by what I wear. Even if I don't follow the practices of those who wear those things, I have made a choice to publicly identify with them. There is no difference between doing that and wearing a swastika. The principle is to not take on the identifying markings of those who don't serve God."

> This is why there is no such thing as a Christian gangster or a Christian Goth. The core beliefs of gangs and Goths oppose the message of the gospel. They are rooted in rebellion and death. You can apply this to many countercultural groups out there. Slapping the name of Jesus on rebellion doesn't make it good. It doesn't make it holy. Isaiah 65:2–6 says: I have stretched out My hands all day long to a rebellious people, who walk in a way that is not good, *according to their own thoughts*; a people who provoke Me to anger continually to My face; who sacrifice in gardens, and burn incense on altars of brick; who sit among the graves, and spend the night in the tombs; who eat swine's flesh, and the broth of abominable things is in their vessels; who say, "Keep to yourself, do not come near me, *for I am holier than you*!" These are smoke in My nostrils, a fire that burns all the day. Behold, it is written before Me: I will not keep silence, but will repay— even repay into their bosom.
>
> —EMPHASIS ADDED

Let's look at these verses one by one, for there is great revelation here. First, God said these people—His people—walk in a way that is not good: "according to their own thoughts" (v. 2). Yet they thought they were pleasing God. They committed these offenses to His face, but these people weren't in willful rebellion against God. They were deceived into believing their practices were good. They not only thought they were doing good but also that they were more holy than those who didn't follow the same practices—"Who say, 'Keep to yourself, do not come near me, for I am holier than you!'" (v. 5).

What were they doing that displeased God so much He said they were "smoke in My nostrils, a fire that burns all the day" and said He "will not keep silence, but will repay"? Verses 3 and 4 give us the answer. The Bible says they were "a people who provoke Me to anger continually to My face; who sacrifice in gardens, and burn incense on altars of brick; who sit among the graves, and spend the night in the tombs; who eat swine's flesh, and the broth of abominable things is in their vessels."

If you study this passage, you will see that the children of Israel were imitating the heathen worship practices of the surrounding nations. They thought they could present themselves to God in the same manner as the ungodly and still be acceptable. They changed their worship practices to match the culture that surrounded them.

Throughout Jewish history we see this time and time again—God's people trying to fit in with the culture of the day and using heathen practices to worship God. Often they just wanted to be like everyone else. They just wanted to fit in. In Moses's day they wanted a graven image because the other nations worshiped idols made of wood and stone. (See Exodus 32.) In Samuel's day they wanted a king because the other nations were led by men, not God. (See 1 Samuel 8.) Again and again God's people were tempted by insecurity and inferiority. They wanted to be like the culture without completely abandoning God. So they incorporated the world's practices into their worship of God.

This has also happened throughout church history with equally devastating results. The Catholic Church, in an attempt to relate to the heathens, incorporated statues and prayers to the dead (the saints).[1] These were heathen practices that the church slapped Jesus's name on in an attempt to relate and identify with the culture around them. All of this flies in the face of God and His Word. He is a jealous God, and He wants to be the sole target of our affections. Deuteronomy 6:5 says, "You shall love the LORD your God with all your heart, with all your soul, and with all your strength." And in the Book of Exodus, God commands us to put nothing above Him.

> You shall have no other gods before Me. You shall not make for yourself a carved image, or any likeness of anything that is in heaven above, or that is in the earth beneath, or that is in the water under the earth; you shall not bow down to them nor serve them. *For I, the LORD your God, am a jealous God.*
>
> —EXODUS 20:3–5, EMPHASIS ADDED

God wants us to find our identity in Him and Him alone. The Bible says in Deuteronomy 6, "And these words which I command you today shall be in your heart.... You shall bind them as a sign on your hand, and they shall be as frontlets between your eyes" (vv. 6, 8). God wants His people to publicly, visibly, and clearly be identified with Him and His Word.

As I said before, you will defend, protect, and promote the thing that forms your identity. Too often God's people are getting their identity from anything and everything other than Christ. This will only lead them farther down the path of bondage to insecurity and inferiority.

I have transgressed the commandment of the Lord and your
words, because I feared the people and obeyed their voice.
—1 SAMUEL 15:24, EMPHASIS ADDED

INSECURITY AND INFERIORITY have torn many great men of God from their positions of honor and anointing. They start so strong and humble before God, but their lives end in destruction. We have seen this throughout history. So many anointed and appointed servants of God ended up eating from the tree, to their own demise. Probably one of the best examples in Scripture is in the story of Saul and David.

Saul had been anointed king over Israel, and the Spirit of God was upon him (1 Sam. 9:15–16; 10:1). But Saul was ruled by insecurity and inferiority. He was so insecure about his position within the hearts of the people that he became a slave to the fear of man. Eventually that led to Saul's undoing. In 1 Samuel 15, God commanded Saul to attack the Amalekites and destroy everything—every man, woman, child, and animal. But Saul did not obey the command of God.

> And Saul attacked the Amalekites, from Havilah all the way to Shur, which is east of Egypt. He also took Agag king of the Amalekites alive, and utterly destroyed all the people with the edge of the sword. But Saul and the people spared Agag and the best of the sheep, the oxen, the fatlings, the lambs, and all

> that was good, and were unwilling to utterly destroy
> them. But everything despised and worthless, that
> they utterly destroyed.
>
> —1 SAMUEL 15:7–9

Saul utterly destroyed all the Amalekites except one: Agag, their king. And he killed all the weak and worthless animals but spared the best. Saul just couldn't bring himself to destroy all the plunder, not when the people would look up to him for bringing home such desirable spoils. So he disregarded God's command.

When Saul reported the results of the battle to Samuel, he told the prophet that he had "performed the commandment of the LORD" (1 Sam. 15:13). But Samuel couldn't be fooled. God had already shown him that Saul did not obey His orders (v. 10). When Samuel confronted Saul, pointing out that he could hear the oxen and sheep, Saul took yet another bite of the fruit of the tree.

> But Samuel said, "What then is this bleating of the
> sheep in my ears, and the lowing of the oxen which
> I hear?" And Saul said, "*They* have brought them
> from the Amalekites; for *the people* spared the best
> of the sheep and the oxen, to sacrifice to the LORD
> your God; and the rest we have utterly destroyed."
>
> —1 SAMUEL 15:14–15, EMPHASIS ADDED

Saul attempted to make excuses and justify his disobedience. He claimed the best animals were spared to use as sacrifices to God. But God didn't ask for animals to sacrifice; He told Saul to destroy everything. On top of that, Saul blamed the people for his disobedience, as if he were not the commanding officer.

This blame-shifting reminds me of someone else. Adam did the same thing in the Garden of Eden when he said, "The woman whom You gave to be with me, she gave me of the tree, and I ate" (Gen. 3:12). Just as Adam blamed Eve, Saul blamed the people of Israel. Then he attempted to minimize his disobedience by pointing out the ways he did obey God.

Those of us who have children know this routine well. How often have we heard our children say, "But I *mostly* obeyed"? Just as we parents do with our children, Samuel pressed Saul to expose the reality of his sin. But Saul remained insistent that he was innocent and that the people took the plunder.

> And Saul said to Samuel, *"But I have obeyed the voice of the LORD*, and gone on the mission on which the LORD sent me, and brought back Agag king of Amalek; I have utterly destroyed the Amalekites. *But the people took of the plunder,* sheep and oxen, the best of the things which should have been utterly destroyed, to sacrifice to the LORD your God in Gilgal."
>
> —1 SAMUEL 15:20–21, EMPHASIS ADDED

After Samuel pressed Saul a third time and delivered to him the word of the Lord, Saul finally admitted his guilt and even the reason for his disobedience. Saul told Samuel, "I have transgressed the commandment of the LORD and your words, *because I feared the people and obeyed their voice*" (1 Sam. 15:24, emphasis added).

This was the beginning of the end for King Saul. He was so insecure about his relationship with the people that instead of commanding them to destroy *all* the Amalekites and spoils, he cowered to their desires and ended up disobeying God. The same thing has happened time and again throughout history.

Saul gave Satan a foothold when he listened to his lies and didn't trust that because God had placed him in position as king, He could keep him there. Instead Saul reached for the fruit of the fear of man, then disobedience. He fell to political pressure and ended up losing his standing with God.

The root of insecurity was now firmly established in Saul,

and he had to pay a painful consequence: the Spirit of God departed from Saul, who desperately wanted to keep his kingdom. Onto this scene now comes God's newly anointed servant David. The hand and favor of God were mightily upon David. He won the battle against Goliath and was becoming a great warrior in Saul's army. You would think this would have made Saul happy. But the person controlled by insecurity and inferiority will grab for some fruit from the tree. Saul became enraged by the attention David was receiving from the people.

> And the women answered one another as they played, and said, Saul hath slain his thousands, and David his ten thousands. And Saul was very wroth, and the saying displeased him; and he said, They have ascribed unto David ten thousands, and to me they have ascribed but thousands: and what can he have more but the kingdom? And Saul eyed David from that day and forward.
>
> And…there was a javelin in Saul's hand. And Saul cast the javelin; for he said, I will smite David even to the wall with it. And David avoided out of his presence twice. And Saul was afraid of David [insecurity], because the LORD was with him [inferiority], and was departed from Saul. Therefore Saul removed him from him.
>
> —1 SAMUEL 18:7–13, KJV

Saul began to compare himself to David, and insecurity and inferiority walked right through that door. Saul began to fear that David would steal the kingdom from him and viewed young David as a threat to his security, value, and stature. And from that point on Saul plotted to kill David.

I wish I could say this kind of jealousy was confined to Bible times, but throughout the ministry today you will find example after example of this very thing happening. Ministers have become afraid another preacher will steal their ministry from them. They are believing a lie. And it affects how they operate, whom they surround themselves with, and how they treat others.

There are also many young ministers who are filled with insecurity and inferiority. They believe older pastors aren't giving them the ministry opportunities they should receive. They feel these older leaders aren't opening doors for them, so they start to grab the fruit of a critical spirit.

On and on it goes. God's leaders keep believing lies from the serpent that make them feel insecure and/or inferior. With fruit in hand, the enemy skillfully presents it to the leaders, and once again they partake of it. There are times and seasons when those of us in ministry realize there is something wrong with our attitude and behavior. We seem to repent, but because we never get to the root issue and only recognize the fruit, the problem comes back. This is also what happened to Saul.

Saul's son Jonathan had what we now might call an intervention. He came to Saul and told him to stop hunting David down because David hadn't done anything to him. Jonathan reminded Saul of all the good David had done, and the prince's words seemed to get through to Saul.

> Thus Jonathan spoke well of David to Saul his father, and said to him, "Let not the king sin against his servant, against David, because he has not sinned against you, and because his works have been very good toward you. For he took his life in his hands and killed the Philistine, and the LORD brought about a great deliverance for all Israel. You saw it and rejoiced. Why then will you sin against innocent blood, to kill David without a cause?" So Saul heeded the voice of Jonathan, and Saul swore, "As the LORD lives, he shall not be killed." Then Jonathan called David, and Jonathan told him all

> these things. So Jonathan brought David to Saul,
> and he was in his presence as in times past.
> —1 SAMUEL 19:4–7

Saul recognized he was wrong and changed his ways—
for a season. As soon as war broke out again and David was
victorious in battle, insecurity got the best of Saul, and he was
again on David's trail, trying to kill him.

> And there was war again: and David went out, and
> fought with the Philistines, and slew them with
> a great slaughter; and they fled from him.... And
> Saul sought to smite David even to the wall with
> the javelin; but he slipped away out of Saul's
> presence, and he smote the javelin into the wall:
> and David fled, and escaped that night. Saul also
> sent messengers unto David's house, to watch
> him, and to slay him in the morning: and Michal
> David's wife told him, saying, If thou save not thy
> life tonight, to morrow thou shalt be slain.
> —1 SAMUEL 19:8, 10–11, KJV

Saul made a pledge to not harm David. Then David began
to walk in his anointing again, and Saul returned to his old
ways. Saul, filled with rage, again tried to kill David because
he never dealt with the roots of insecurity and inferiority, even
though on several occasions he admitted that what he was
doing was wrong and offered what seemed to be repentance.

Saul's life reflects so many today. They start out under the
anointing but end up believing a lie. They fall prey because in
their hearts there was an open door to insecurity and inferiority. We must go deep into the spirit to the root cause if we
are truly going to be free.

8

THE TRAPPED CHRISTIAN

Therefore if the Son makes you free, you shall be free indeed.
—JOHN 8:36

A s GOD HAS continued to unveil this amazing truth into my life, I see the working of insecurity and inferiority in almost every facet of life. I see in my own life the many arenas where it plays such a major role, yet often in a stealth way. Because these two demon spirits are the footholds of many other spirits, often we only see the most visible ones and not the roots.

In the vision God gave me, I could see the two tentacles to which all the other spirits were attached, but I was unable to identify them until I went much deeper in the Spirit. I clearly saw the names of the demons of fear, hate, lust, rage, drugs, and so on. However, it wasn't until I pressed in much deeper in the Spirit that my eyes were opened, and I saw under the surface to the real roots that gave all these other spirits strength.

I have found that this vision was so accurate in revealing to me not only what the root spirits were but also how hidden and hard to identify they so often are. Many Christians struggle and fight with so many strongholds. They go to church, read books, receive prayer, even attend deliverance services, but so often they continue to struggle with fear, anger, rage, lust, pornography, homosexuality, unforgiveness, greed, intimidation, and many other issues.

We often see people come into the church with these

struggles and never truly get free. They come for a while and then usually end up in one of three camps. The first camp is the camp of condemnation. The people in this camp go to a church that preaches righteous and holy living. They know the Word they are receiving is the truth but can never seem to get it to work out in their own lives. Try as they may, they live in a state of continual condemnation, always feeling unworthy and unable to obtain victory. But because of their love for God and/or their fear of hell, they remain in the church, often putting on the mask of religion so nobody sees the struggles they are going through.

The second group also continues in a church, but they find one that preaches a gospel of "grace." The grace these Christians follow after is not true grace but a license to sin. They hear messages about how to have a successful career and how to keep a positive attitude, but they're never challenged to confront strongholds that may be at work in their lives. The church avoids pointing out the spiritual strongholds and often justifies them with a doctrine that says, "As long as we're in the flesh, we can't be free from sin." Although this kind of teaching brings freedom from the feelings of condemnation, it doesn't bring the freedom Christ died for us to experience.

The third group of people is the largest. They simply give up. They stop trying to fight and eventually leave the church all together. Many believe the church is an outdated, irrelevant institution that doesn't have any real answers for them. Unfortunately, in some ways they're right. Oh, the gospel has all the answers and is truly relevant, but what many churches present today isn't the full gospel.

I once attended a major black charismatic church in the Chicago area. The music was high-powered and the atmosphere electrified. Every month they would have a deliverance service. Now, I believe in the delivering power of God, and God has used me to cast demons out of hundreds of people. I have seen, in a single service, more than two hundred people manifest demons, and at the name of Jesus all two hundred were instantly delivered. However, in this service the regular church members who had been prayed for over and over again all came for another "deliverance." They showed up with their little brown paper bags so they could throw up the demons.

You would hear the people start to choke and cough, some even gag. They would go through this ritual month after month but never seem to get truly free. The Word is clear: "Therefore if the Son makes you free, you shall be free indeed" (John 8:36). I'm not saying these people aren't wrestling with demonic powers, but where is the freedom? Is it possible that, just like in my vision, they keep going after the surface spirits and fail to deal with the real root demons that were giving them strength?

I want to address an issue here. When I talk about these demonic powers having access to our lives because of insecurity and inferiority, I am not necessarily saying these demons possess us. I am speaking of the kind of demonic influence that all of us face all the time. Although demon possession is real and needs to be dealt with, most of what we wrestle with as Christians falls under the category of the works of the flesh. (See Galatians 5:19–21.) These are those things that are the result of the fall of man and the working of sin. They are, however, fueled by the demon powers at work in the world. As the apostle Paul wrote, "For we wrestle not against flesh and blood, but against principalities, against powers, against the rulers of the darkness of this world, against spiritual wickedness in high places" (Eph. 6:12, KJV).

Our fight is both internal and external. It's this one-two punch that confuses and holds so many believers captive. The enemy knows that unless he can gain a foothold in someone's thinking, he cannot truly control that person. Satan has no strength over us as believers except the power we give him when we submit to and agree with his lies. The battlefield is twofold and must be fought on both fronts. It is in the heavenlies, and it is in our minds.

9

THE KEYS TO SUCCESSFUL WARFARE

*For the weapons of our warfare are not carnal, but mighty
through God to the pulling down of strong holds.*
—2 CORINTHIANS 10:4–5, KJV

TRUE FREEDOM IN Christ will come only when we learn
how to wage successful spiritual warfare. In order to do
that, we need a revelation of two things: the location of
our enemy and the location of the battlefield. In other words,
we must know whom we're fighting and where the battle is.

Just take the United States' war on terror for example. This
has been a most difficult war because the two primary elements
of successful warfare are so hard to clearly identify. First, we
had a hard time locating our enemy. It took the United States
years to locate Osama bin Laden. He evaded capture for nearly
a decade after 9/11 before US Special Forces killed him in a raid
on his compound in 2011. But we still had a second problem.

The death of Osama bin Laden did not remove the threat
of al Qaeda. There are still terrorist cells all over the world
filled with brainwashed militants who want to destroy America
and Israel. We don't know where in the world the next battle
is going to be fought. Will they attack New York again with
planes, an embassy in Africa with car bombs, or a crowded
marketplace in the Middle East? There are so many ways they
can attack with little or no warning.

America has the power to destroy our enemy, but if we can't
locate him and the battlefield, we will never succeed in the war

on terror. If we can't locate these two key areas, we will never be free. This is why we spend so much time and resources gathering *intelligence*. Intelligence is the key to winning the war. If we get the right intelligence, we can win. If not, we are still vulnerable.

All truth is parallel. The same is true in spiritual warfare. We need spiritual intelligence. If we can locate our enemy and the battlefield, we can easily defeat our enemy. We already have overwhelming firepower through the blood of Jesus. The Bible tells us in Luke 10:19 that we have been given authority to trample on serpents and scorpions, and over all the power of the enemy, and nothing shall by any means hurt us. This is why Satan is terrified of you discovering his best-kept secrets—insecurity and inferiority—and these two keys to spiritual warfare.

Now that we have located our deeply hidden enemy, we are halfway to victory. The second key is to find the battlefield. This is revealed to us in 2 Corinthians:

> (For the weapons of our warfare are not carnal, but mighty through God to the pulling down of strong holds;) casting down imaginations, and every high thing that exalteth itself against the knowledge of God, and *bringing into captivity every thought* to the obedience of Christ.
>
> —2 Corinthians 10:4–5, kjv, emphasis added

The battlefield is in our minds. Despite all the warfare the enemy wages in the atmosphere (Eph. 6:12), if he has no access to our minds, we will have total victory. If we can win in the battle of the mind, we can win the battle of life. Satan sets up strongholds in our thought life. It's the *same* strategy he used on Eve in the garden. He didn't have the power to take her captive. He had to convince her to willingly surrender herself to his control and influence. He had to cause her to want to follow him. He had to plant seeds into her mind that she would act on—thoughts that were lies.

She had to become *deceived*. If he could only convince her of his lie, then he could lead her into a path of destruction and bondage through disobedience. He needed to establish a *stronghold* in her mind.

> Now the serpent was more subtil than any beast of the field which the LORD God had made. And he said unto the woman, Yea, hath God said, Ye shall not eat of every tree of the garden? And the woman said unto the serpent, We may eat of the fruit of the trees of the garden: But of the fruit of the tree which is in the midst of the garden, God hath said, Ye shall not eat of it, neither shall ye touch it, lest ye die. And the serpent said unto the woman, *Ye shall not surely die* [stronghold of insecurity]: For God doth know that in the day ye eat thereof, then your eyes shall be opened, and *ye shall be as gods* [stronghold of inferiority], knowing good and evil. And when the woman saw that the tree was good for food, and that it was pleasant to the eyes, and a tree to be *desired to make one wise* [Eve was now deceived. She believed the lie that the tree was good and pleasant and desirable], she took of the fruit thereof, and did eat, and gave also unto her husband with her; and he did eat.
> —GENESIS 3:1–6, KJV, EMPHASIS ADDED

There were three results of deception that led Eve down the path of destruction:

1. She *felt* that the fruit was *good*.

2. She *felt* that the fruit would be *pleasant*.

3. She *felt* that the fruit was something to be
   desired.

All three of these *feelings* were lies. The tree was never good for man. It has led to thousands of years of death, destruction, and chaos. But these three things reveal to us an amazing truth about human nature: we gravitate toward pleasure and flee from pain. God made us that way. Even in the garden He warned Adam and Eve of the *pain* of disobedience:

> And the woman said unto the serpent, We may eat
> of the fruit of the trees of the garden: But of the
> fruit of the tree which is in the midst of the garden,
> *God* hath said, Ye shall not eat of it, *neither shall ye
> touch it, lest ye die.*
> —Genesis 3:2–3, kjv, emphasis added

Satan's strategy was to get Eve to believe a lie because he knew that once she believed the lie, her emotions would begin to lead her down a wrong path. For years preachers have said that we are not to live according to feelings. This is a fallacy. Mankind has always been driven by his emotions and always will be. Emotions are our primary source of motivation and energy. Scientists say that 70 percent of our physical energy comes from our emotions.[1] We are *not* to deny our emotions. We are to make sure they are moving us toward godly things and not the works of the flesh.

Emotions are all rooted in thoughts. Your thoughts determine what you feel. If what you think is correct, then what you feel will be correct. If your thinking is wrong, then your feelings will be wrong. Eve started to think through the eyes of insecurity and inferiority. She believed God had lied to her and was withholding something good from her. She felt pain, and she wanted to feel pleasure again. She felt that if she ate the fruit of the forbidden tree, she would be free from the pain of insecurity and inferiority and have pleasure once again. She was deceived. What she felt was based upon her wrong thinking.

PLEASURE AND PAIN

We have so much to learn from Eve! This strategy of Satan continues today. Satan uses the pain from insecurity and inferiority, and our intense desire to alleviate that pain and acquire the pleasure of security and worth, to get us to follow him to do almost anything. If the feelings of pain for not doing something and the desire to experience pleasure by doing it are strong enough, we will do just about anything.

We see this even in the horrible tragedy of suicide. Somewhere in the person's mind he has become convinced that the pain of living is greater than the potential pain of killing himself and that the pleasure of being free from the pressures of this life is greater than the pleasure of living. Because of this distorted view of pleasure and pain, the person becomes willing to kill himself. The deception has gone so deep that the individual is willing to engage in such a destructive form of escapism. People do this to a lesser degree all the time. They escape into drugs, alcohol, sex, pornography, riotous living, and the like to be free from pain or to experience pleasure.

People are drawn toward these self-destructive pursuits because they become convinced that even though morally wrong, these activities are actually *good* for them. They believe these things will give them *pleasure* and therefore are to be *desired*. Even Christians fall into this trap all the time. Perhaps the sin isn't drug addiction or fornication but something as small as overeating. They know that extra doughnut won't do them any good. They know overeating can lead to serious health problems and even early death. But they look at that food and say, "This is good, pleasant, and desirable." If you withhold it from them, they will feel deprived.

These Christians have come to believe the enemy's lie that giving in to their desires is good because it will give them pleasure. Yet instead of feeling good, they become trapped in an endless cycle of defeat. They diet but to no avail. Then they begin to fundamentally believe that all that unhealthy food they're eating is good, pleasant, and desirable.

I have heard from pulpits for years that sin is *fun*, that it is pleasant and enjoyable, but we are supposed to deny ourselves. We have this thing all wrong. If you have the mind of Christ, then sin will never seem fun to you. It will never seem pleasant. It will never seem enjoyable. The Bible declares, "Therefore, if anyone is in Christ, he is a new creation; old things have passed away; behold, all things have become new" (2 Cor. 5:17). And it says, "Let this mind be in you, which was also in Christ Jesus" (Phil. 2:5, kjv). And again the Bible says in 1 Peter 4:1, "Therefore, since Christ suffered for us in the flesh, *arm yourselves also with the same mind*, for he who has suffered in the flesh has ceased from sin" (emphasis added).

Did Jesus look at sin with longing? No, I tell you! He hated sin. He had His mind so in line with the mind of the Father that even His senses were repulsed by sin. We too can live this way. We can so take on the mind of Christ that even our senses, our emotions, are repulsed by sin. Hebrews 5:14 says that "by reason of use" those who are mature "*have their senses exercised to discern both good and evil*" (emphasis added).

I personally have experienced this in my own life. When I was saved, God delivered me from five years of heavy drug and alcohol use. He not only broke the power of the physical addiction off my life, but He also forever removed the desire. I have never even wanted to touch a drug since that day. What happened to so totally free me that I would never return to that which used to dominate my life? I had an experience! I had an experience with the living Word that was so overwhelming, so strong, so good, pleasant, and desirable that it forever changed the way I think.

Once I experienced the living reality of Christ deep enough, I longed for Him more than for the drugs. I saw Christ as the thing to be desired and felt that being without Him would be horribly painful. My emotions were now forever changed. What I used to long for I now had a disdain for. In one night I was forever changed. In one night my emotions stopped driving me into sin and bondage and turned to drive me into the loving arms of Christ. I now thought differently; therefore I felt different. Therefore I acted different. Satan had lost his hold on me.

If you are going to walk in total victory, you must be able to locate your enemy and locate the battlefield. Your greatest enemy is wrong thinking, and the battlefield is your mind. You may say, "I thought Satan was my greatest enemy." He is your enemy, but he has been defeated. If he can't get you to believe a lie, then he has *no* power over you at all. He is powerless to touch you if you have right, godly thinking.

Satan's strategy hasn't changed throughout history. It is exactly the same. He wants to get you to believe a lie so you will feel insecure and inferior. Then as those negative emotions begin to pulsate through your being, he will present to you another lie. He will show you something bad and convince you it is good, pleasant, and desirable to remove your insecurity and your inferiority. Once you take a bite of his fruit, you have entered his trap and reinforced his control over your life.

10

TRUE AND FALSE REPENTANCE

For godly sorrow worketh repentance to salvation not to be repented of: but the sorrow of the world worketh death.

—2 CORINTHIANS 7:10, KJV

TAKING EVERY THOUGHT captive is the key to total victory. Scripture commands us to repent. Repenting is not necessarily boohooing and crying, snotting and spitting everywhere. I have seen a lot of people go through the emotional expressions of so-called repentance but never change. Once again they have fallen into the trap of wrong emotions based upon wrong thinking.

Often when the Lord truly deals deeply with you, there is a great flood of emotions, including intense sorrow and remorse, for the sin in which you've been involved. But many people think that just because they experienced a flood tide of emotions, they have repented. We say they are "broken." Pastors get excited when they see this, church members rejoice, and the person under conviction feels like he is now right with God.

All of this is a great deception because, as of yet, this person hasn't repented. Although this expression of sorrow and remorse can be, and often is, the first step toward repentance, it isn't repentance in itself. Second Corinthians 7:10 says, "For godly sorrow produces repentance leading to salvation, not to be regretted; but the sorrow of the world produces death."

Sorrow leads us to repentance, but sorrow isn't repentance. True repentance isn't an emotional display. It's a change in the way we think. The Greek word for *repent* means to change one's thinking, to think differently.[1] In order for genuine repentance to take place, there must be a fundamental change in the way one thinks. If a person doesn't change the way he thinks, he will ultimately never change his actions. His emotional desire to experience pleasure and avoid pain will continue to drive him. And he will once again fall into the trap of Satan.

Often I have seen people come into church and be greatly moved upon by the Spirit of the Lord. God genuinely convicts them of their sin, and they are overcome by deep feelings of regret and sorrow. The church members come up and hug them at the altar and say things like "Praise God, you're saved" or "You've rededicated your life to Christ." The repentant people feel loved and accepted. They like this feeling, so they come back to the next church service. Although they still may not have fundamentally changed the way they think about sin, they might be willing to avoid some overt sins, because they want to be accepted by this new church peer group. They start going through all the motions of religion, believing all along that they are born again.

They are feeling a new sense of security and value because of the peer acceptance. But because the change is only outward and not inward, they are not experiencing new life in Christ. Instead they are beginning to eat of the fruit of religion. If the desire for the acceptance of man is deep enough, and if enough of their value and security comes from this new group of church friends, they will be willing to change even more of their outward behavior.

All along they are being driven by this need for security and value, not by power of the Holy Spirit. If they get that sense of worth from the church group, they will stay in the church to feed this need. If their unsaved friends satisfy this need for acceptance more than the church group does, they will quickly return to their old lifestyle.

This happens because true repentance never actually took place. The person simply started to eat a different piece of fruit from the same deceptive tree. Deep inside they still love sin and are bound by the trap of the tree. Insecurity and inferiority rule their emotional lives, thus dictating their actions.

ROTTEN FRUIT

In my years as a pastor and evangelist, I have seen many people come and stay in church for a season. The church preaches surrender to God and an ever-deepening commitment to holy living, which starts producing a conflict within them. Although they love the sense of security and value they get from church, they start feeling condemned. They are being convicted but still aren't repentant. They aren't willing to change the way they think about sin. So they try to behave. But because they can't resist sin in their flesh, these people begin to feel like it's impossible to live a Christian life. This conflict causes them to feel insecure and inferior again, and the enemy steps right in to offer them some fruit.

He offers different pieces to different people. To some he offers the fruit of self-condemnation. These people begin to beat themselves up verbally and mentally, telling themselves, "I'm no good" or "I'm too weak." They begin to think they will never make it and are emotionally driven right back out of the church, thinking the gospel has no real power to change them.

To some the enemy offers the fruit of a critical spirit. These individuals feel insecure and inferior, so they begin to attack the church, its leaders, and its doctrine. They love to call Christians legalistic and judgmental. They love to think the problem is with everybody else. They say the congregation isn't loving enough, the pastor is too harsh, or no one understands what they are going through. These believers will often leave and go to a church that "accepts them as they are." This usually refers to a church that won't preach holiness and doesn't require righteous living but rather a "grace" that doesn't require holiness.

Some will remain in their original church and will gather a small group that agrees with them that the leadership is harsh and unloving. This new group will help bolster their negative feelings about the church. In both instances, these critical churchgoers are being driven by insecurity and inferiority. They simply pick up a different piece of fruit to provide for themselves the feelings of security and value they seek.

To some Satan offers the fruit of rebellion. These individuals just blatantly begin to reject the Word of God and the teachings of the church. They run back to their old lifestyles and to friends who won't require them to change.

And to others the enemy offers the fruit of religion. To deal with their growing feelings of insecurity and inferiority, these individuals hunker down and begin to "deny" their flesh. They'll focus on changing even more outward actions so people will applaud them for having "grown in the Lord." They'll attend every church service, change their dress and speech, pay their tithes, and do all their religious duties. Not only this, but they become zealots for outward expressions of holiness.

They'll begin to preach to everyone about their newfound convictions and belittle other churchgoers for not conforming. This newfound zeal feeds them with a sense of superiority and deepens their bondage. These "preachers of holiness" make young Christians and anyone who doesn't measure up to their standards their whipping posts. Depending on the church or organization they belong to, these "super saints" may start being promoted to leadership positions. People within the church who also are getting their sense of security and value from their outward righteousness will recognize the "call of God" on these people's lives and empower them to climb even further up the ranks of church hierarchy. The trap of the tree goes on and on.

Those who leave the church are now convinced that there is no real power inside the church to change them. The fact is they never really repented. The trap of the tree goes on and on.

TRUE REPENTANCE

True repentance isn't a feeling; it's an action. It is to change the way one thinks. If you think in accordance with the Word of God, then your feelings and emotions will line up with the Word of God and drive you in the right direction. That is why Scripture makes some very powerful statements about the person who has truly repented and been born again.

> Whoever has been born of God *does not sin*, for His seed remains in him; and *he cannot sin*, because he has been born of God.
> —1 JOHN 3:9, EMPHASIS ADDED

The Amplified Bible says it this way: "No one born (begotten) of God [deliberately, knowingly, and habitually] practices sin."

One day while I was driving to a meeting in Sacramento, California, the Spirit of God began to speak to me about sin. He gave me a definition of sin that forever changed my life and has changed the lives of multitudes around the world who have heard me share it. The Holy Spirit said, "*The essence of sin is the rejection of God's rightful authority over one's life.*"

Everything in the kingdom of heaven is about authority. The word *authority* in the Greek refers to the *legal right to exercise power*.[2] When someone has authority, he has the legal right to exercise power over another. Let me give you a real-world example.

My brother is a California Highway Patrol officer. One of the areas he patrols is the I-5 corridor through parts of central California. When he sees a motorist speeding, he will quickly catch up to the driver and turn on that infamous red light.

Most of the time the speeding motorist slows down and stops on the side of the road. My brother will get out of his car, and, as most of us have experienced, he will ask the motorist for his driver's license and registration. The driver, without question, will hand the documents over to my brother.

Why? Is my brother intimidating? He is six feet tall but not that physically intimidating. The driver gives my brother what he asked for because he recognizes that my brother has a legal right to pull him over and ask for his documentation. He submits to my brother's legal right of authority.

The motorist isn't coerced or without a choice, like some kind of robot. There came a moment when he made a decision. When the speeding driver saw the lights on my brother's car, he had a choice to make. He had to ask himself, "Do I accept this officer's legal right of authority, or do I reject it?"

If the motorist were to reject my brother's legal authority, he could react in any number of ways. He could keep driving and simply ignore the light. He could try to speed away or even ram my brother's police car. He could pull over, jump out of his car, and start cursing at my brother or even try to attack him. But before he could choose to do any of those things, he first would have to decide that he wasn't going to accept my brother's legal right to pull him over.

Sin is an authority issue. God created us and has an inherent right to tell us what to do, what to say, and how to live. He is Lord. From the beginning all sin has been based in this single first step: *the rejection of God's rightful authority over our lives.* Lucifer in heaven had to first reject God's rightful authority before he could even consider defying Him.

The same is true with us. In order to disobey God, we must first reject His legal right of authority over us. We must say, "*No,* I will not submit to You. I reject Your legal, rightful claims over my life and actions." Oh, we might not say it that boldly, but we all do it. You can't commit any act of disobedience until you first reject God's legal, rightful authority over your life.

THE ESSENCE OF SIN

Now, the Bible commands us to repent of our sins. In other words, we are to change the way we think about rejecting God's rightful authority and accept His right to rule and reign in our lives. This is true repentance. That is why 1 John 3:9 says, "No one born (begotten) of God [deliberately, knowingly, and habitually] practices sin" (AMP), or rejects God's rightful authority. The person who has truly repented has stopped rejecting God's rightful authority and has chosen to submit to Him.

Once a person chooses to submit, then all the power he needs to live according to God's Word is released. When we repent, God will forgive us and *cleanse* us from all unrighteousness. (See 1 John 1:9.) He will cleanse us from all our ungodlike character and create in us His character and nature. The power of sin over our lives will be broken. As we take each area of our lives to God and surrender it to the rightful authority of Christ, the power of redemption and deliverance will begin to work practically in our daily actions.

It really makes sense if you think about it. If I have truly repented, I have changed my thinking about rejecting God's rightful authority over a particular issue in my life. So now I not only submit to God, but I also agree with Him that the particular act is utterly sinful and abhorrent. My belief about the desirability of that particular sin now has changed. At this point my feelings about this sin change from desire to disgust— from longing for it to wanting to leave it alone. As long as I agree with God's perspective of this sin, I will feel God's way about it. My emotions will then be godlike emotions and will drive me away from that sinful behavior.

If you are still being drawn toward certain sins, it is because

you have *not* truly and completely repented. You may feel very
guilty and ashamed of your desires, but deep down you still
love them. Deep down that sin is feeding some area of insecurity or inferiority, and the desire to satisfy those feelings
is greater than your willingness to submit to God's rightful
authority in your life. The only way to be free is to truly repent
and surrender to God's authority in your life.

11

SATAN'S ENDGAME

And [the serpent] said to the woman, "Has God indeed said, 'You shall not eat of every tree of the garden'?"
—GENESIS 3:1

A S WE DISCOVERED in the last chapter, everything in the kingdom of heaven is about authority. I want to take you much deeper in the Spirit so you can gain an understanding of how the enemy operates in the areas of insecurity and inferiority. Let's once again go back to the original fall of man in the Book of Genesis.

> Now the serpent was more cunning than any beast of the field which the LORD God had made. And he said to the woman, "Has God indeed said, 'You shall not eat of every tree of the garden'?" And the woman said to the serpent, "We may eat the fruit of the trees of the garden; but of the fruit of the tree which is in the midst of the garden, God has said, 'You shall not eat it, nor shall you touch it, lest you die.'"
>
> Then the serpent said to the woman, "You will not surely die. For God knows that in the day you eat of it your eyes will be opened, and you will be like God, knowing good and evil." So when the woman saw that the tree was good for food, that it was pleasant to the eyes, and a tree desirable to

make one wise, she took of its fruit and ate. She
also gave to her husband with her, and he ate.

—GENESIS 3:1–6

When we look at this story, we must ask ourselves a couple
of key questions. What was the enemy's endgame in releasing
these two demon spirits upon Eve? What was he trying to
accomplish? I submit to you that Satan was after only one
thing: breaking the authority relationship between man and
God.

Satan, better than any other creature, understood the issue
of authority. He knew that authority is never taken; it is only
given. I want you to put that truth deep inside your spirit.
Authority is never taken; it is only given. You do not have the
right to exercise authority unless you are under authority. Satan
understood that all the power Adam and Eve had on the earth
came solely from their authority relationship with God—that
God had given them that power and the right to exercise it
here on the earth. God had given Adam and Eve dominion.

The Bible tells us in Genesis 1:28, "Then God blessed them,
and God said to them, 'Be fruitful and multiply; fill the earth
and subdue it; have dominion over the fish of the sea, over
the birds of the air, and over every living thing that moves
on the earth.'" When you look at the verse, you'll notice the
first thing God gave to Adam and Eve was the power of the
blessing. The blessing is not things such as new cars, clothes, or
money. It is the power to prosper. So often we refer to something we receive unexpectedly as a blessing, but the blessing is
the anointing, favor, and power of God that give us the ability
to prosper in every area of our lives.

God set His blessing on Adam and Eve and told them to
be fruitful. As they were fruitful they were to multiply, causing
them to fill the earth, subdue it, and have dominion. God gave
Adam and Eve dominion over the fish of the sea, over the birds
of the air, and over every living thing that moved on the earth.

Man had the legal right to exercise power over everything on the earth. That is what authority is. *Exousia,* the Greek word for authority, literally means the right to exercise power.[1] God had given Adam and Eve the legal right to exercise power here on the earth. He gave them dominion.

Lucifer had dominion in heaven. He was the highest of all created beings. He was the guardian cherub. He had incredible power and authority in heaven. But when he rejected God's authority and tried to raise himself up and take over heaven, he lost the dominion power he had. (See Isaiah 14:12–14.)

We need to get a revelation here. You can still have your giftings, your talents, and your abilities but have lost your dominion power. This is what the serpent was after in the Garden of Eden. He wanted Eve to reject God's legal right of authority over her life and thereby lose her dominion power. After Adam and Eve fell, they no longer had dominion over the fish of the sea, over the birds of the air, and over every living thing that moved on the earth. When they rejected God's legal right of authority in their lives, they lost the dominion power they were supposed to operate in.

Satan knew that if he could get Adam and Eve to violate God's law and thereby break the authority relationship they had with God, he could rob them of the power and position God had given them. I want you to put this very deep in your spirit because Jesus came to restore that which the devil has stolen. If you read Matthew 16:15–19, you'll see this truth laid out.

> He said to them, "But who do you say that I am?" Simon Peter answered and said, "You are the Christ, the Son of the living God." Jesus answered and said to him, "Blessed are you, Simon Bar-Jonah, for flesh and blood has not revealed this to you, but My Father who is in heaven. And I also say to you that you are Peter, and on this rock I will build My church, and the gates of Hades shall not

> prevail against it. And I will give you the keys of
> the kingdom of heaven, and whatever you bind on
> earth will be bound in heaven, and whatever you
> loose on earth will be loosed in heaven."

Jesus asked Peter, "Who do you say that I am?" Peter
answered and said, "You are the Christ, the Son of the living
God." And Jesus said to him, "Blessed are you." Why was Peter
blessed? What was the fullness of the revelation that Peter had
just received? Peter told Jesus, "You are the Christ. You are
the Anointed One, the Messiah. You are the Savior and the
authority to come." Peter was saying, "Jesus, I recognize You as
the one anointed and sent by God to be my King."

That's what the Jews were looking for when Jesus arrived
on the scene. They were looking for a new leader anointed and
appointed by God to be their king and lead them to political
victory. That's why they shouted, "Hosanna," when Jesus made
His triumphal entry into Jerusalem during His final week here
on the earth. *Hosanna* means a king is coming.[2] Peter had
received a revelation of who Jesus really was and the authority
He carried. This is why Jesus said, "You are blessed because My
Father in heaven has revealed this to you."

Now let's look at Matthew 16:18. In this verse Jesus is basically telling Peter, "Upon this rock—upon the revelation you
just had of My authority—I will build My church, and the
gates of hell shall not prevail against it. You just got the key to
victory, Peter. You just got the understanding that I've come to
restore the authority and dominion that was lost."

Look at the next verse. Jesus said, "And I will give you
the keys of the kingdom of heaven." A kingdom is a realm
or sphere in which one thing is dominant. It is a place where
an authority or a king rules. Jesus said that once you get this
revelation of His authority and get rightly submitted to His
authority, He will give back to you the dominion power that
was lost in the Garden of Eden. And once He gives you back

that dominion power, the forces of hell shall no longer have any power over you.

Jesus was telling Peter, "I will build My church upon this revelation—the revelation of the kingdom and the restoration of dominion authority and the power that comes when you submit to My Lordship—and the gates of hell shall not prevail against it."

We have already learned that everything in the kingdom of heaven is about authority. Satan's ultimate goal in the garden was to break the authority relationship between man and God. If he could break that relationship, he could rob man of the power of dominion. This is the same thing the enemy is ultimately after when he comes against us with insecurity and inferiority.

PERVERTED PERCEPTION

You may be wondering what made Eve willing to step out from under God's authority in her life. How did Satan get her to violate the authority relationship she had with God? We have no idea how long Adam and Eve were in the garden before this temptation took place. We also have no idea how long the temptation went on. When we read the story in Genesis, we tend to think everything happened in one short conversation, and it very likely did. But it is possible that this was a progressive temptation and that continual communication went on for a period of time. Whatever the case, Satan coaxed Eve into a place where she was willing to violate the authority relationship she had with God and disobey His clear command, which she fully understood.

I've heard many people say the serpent deceived Eve, and this is absolutely true. But the serpent didn't cause Eve to misunderstand the clear-cut command of God. Eve was deceived into thinking her willingness to violate the command of God was justified. Eve understood what was right and wrong, but she embraced a belief system that allowed her to justify in her own mind her decision to reject God's command. The deception changed her perception of reality. Put that in your spirit: *deception changes perception.*

Satan deceived her by bringing into question the truthfulness of God's command. He declared, "You will not surely die." Satan sowed a seed into Eve that got her to question the motives of God. He got Eve to begin to question what God was really after when He gave her this command. He reinforced this when he implied that God was secretly withholding from Adam and Eve something that would greatly benefit them. He told her God knew that when she ate of the tree she would have something He was trying to keep from her—He was trying to withhold a special blessing that would allow her to be just like Him.

Satan caused Eve to believe that the motivation behind God's command not to eat of the tree was a selfish attempt to keep Adam and Eve from being all they could be. This deception changed Eve's perception of reality. When she began to question God's motives, Eve initiated the mental process that enabled her to justify her disobedience and then reject God's authority. This is the very strategy the enemy uses today to wreak havoc not only in our relationship with God but also in our relationships with one another.

We must look at what happened with Eve very carefully. Eve knew the clear command of God. She told Satan that if she ate of the tree or even touched it she would die. The problem began when she started to question God's motives. She began to believe that God's declaration of judgment on the disobedient was not genuine. When the conversation with the serpent began, she believed the tree was bad for her. However, if you look at Genesis 3:6, it is clear that her entire perception of reality has suddenly changed: "So when the woman saw that the tree was good for food, that it was pleasant to the eyes, and a tree desirable to make one wise, she took of its fruit and ate. She also gave to her husband with her, and he ate."

When the woman saw the fruit after questioning God's motives, her perception was different. What she used to believe was bad she now believed was good. What she used to believe was destructive she now believed was pleasant to the eyes. What she used to believe would bring death she now believed would make her wiser and more alive. Her deception, which stemmed from her willingness to believe the lies of the enemy, changed her perception. That's so important I need to say it again. *Eve's deception changed her perception.*

When Eve made a judgment about God's motives, her ability to correctly see the truth became perverted. She could no longer accurately discern truth because she was now sitting on the judgment seat with her authority—God. And that perverted her view of everything God had ever said and would ever say to her. This is the very nature of deception. Deception will pervert your perception of reality.

When Eve believed God's motives were wrong, she then was able to justify in her own mind rejecting God's rightful authority over her life. She now took authority to herself, developed her own perception of reality, and acted freely on this new perspective. It all began when Eve sat on the judgment seat and made a conclusion about the motives of God's heart. This kind of judgment is the root cause of many of our violations of established authority.

People violate authority for two main reasons. The first is out of blatant rebellion. This is when you clearly know the truth and choose to reject it and do your own thing. That is not what happened in the garden. Although Eve's action was rebellious, she did it because she was deceived.

The second reason people violate authority, which is much more common, is because they've come to a false judgment of the motives of an authority, and that perverts their perception of reality. When people get a warped perception of reality, they easily behave in a rebellious way because they feel completely justified in their actions. They do not believe themselves to be rebellious. They do not believe themselves to be in disobedience. They feel fully and completely justified. This happens because they filter the communication of the authority figure through the new perspective of reality developed when they judged that authority's motives.

We see this in every aspect of life. We see this often in the inner cities, where a deep mistrust of police officers is frequently sown into the hearts of young people. They have come to believe that the police are racist and wrongly target certain ethnic groups. They believe police officers are in their neighborhood simply to harass them. When a young person believes this, any interaction he or she has with the police will be filtered through that perception of the police officers' motives.

So if a police officer stops a person and asks to see her license, someone who views law enforcement through this negative lens may get angry and say, "Why are you harassing me?" The police officer was not treating her differently than he would any other citizen. But because that individual already carried a distrust of police officers' motives, she perceived the officer's actions as unjustified harassment. So instead of being respectful and submissive to authority, the person may become argumentative and combative. She may fight back or even try to flee—all the while feeling completely justified in her actions because she believes the police officer's motives are wrong.

We see this in families all the time. The parent tells the teenager he is not allowed to go out to a party. The teenager starts to believe the parents simply want to keep him from having fun. Then he begins to think his parents have something against his friends. When the teenager stops believing his parents' rules are there to protect him and are instead being driven by some other motive, the teen is able to justify the idea of rebelling against his parents' authority.

The enemy loves to get us to judge people's motives. This not only causes individuals to rebel against authority, but it also creates incredible division in relationships.

12

THE JUDGMENT SEAT

*Judge not, that you be not judged. For with what judgment you judge, you will
be judged; and with the measure you use, it will be measured back to you.*

—MATTHEW 7:1–2

T HE ENEMY ASSAULTS us with the spirits of inferiority
and insecurity to destroy many relationships, not just
those between police officers and communities, or
between teenagers and their parents. He uses this process of
causing people to question a person's motives to destroy relationships within the church too. I've seen this happen time and
time again.

Several years ago a friend of mine was invited to join the
staff of a church a minister-friend of his had recently planted.
Bob* was told that he would be groomed to lead the church
when the pastor and co-pastor retired in a few years. After
praying about the offer, Bob felt the Lord leading him to take
the position. So he and his family moved back to his home
state to begin serving in this church.

The church was only a couple of years old. But the founding
pastor was traveling and speaking frequently, and he couldn't
lead the church by himself. So he'd asked a close friend of his,
Tom**, to serve as his co-pastor. Tom had never led a very large
church but had always lived in the shadow of his friend's ministry success. At the time Bob thought nothing of it, but he was

---

* Not his real name
** Not his real name

about to come face-to-face with the devastating, destructive effects of insecurity and inferiority within the leadership of a local church.

When Bob joined the staff of the church, the plan was for him to lead weekly revival services. The pastors put him completely in charge of the revival services, and the power of God moved in an incredible way. The congregation responded very positively. The response was so strong, in fact, that the revival services began to draw a significantly larger crowd than the Sunday services Tom was leading. And this is where everything began to go wrong.

Bob did not realize it, but Tom was becoming extremely fearful and jealous over what God was doing in the revival services. Although he was technically leading the church, Tom began to go behind the scenes and demand that other leaders in the church not attend the services Bob was leading. The fact that the people responded so well to Bob and that he drew larger crowds made Tom feel incredibly insecure and inferior. Soon he began to criticize Bob's preaching and the manifestations of God happening in the revival. And Tom started to belittle those who were attending the services, saying they were shallow Christians just seeking a show.

For several months Bob did not know this was going on, though he was well aware that there was tension between him and Tom. After Bob had been in the church for about four months, Tom stood up in one of the revival services and publicly confessed that he had become jealous of the fact that God was using Bob and didn't seem to be using him. Bob was shocked, as you might imagine, but also very excited that Tom was publicly confessing his sin. He thought they would be able to move forward in ministry together. Unfortunately, this was not going to be the case.

Insecurity and inferiority continued to work in Tom, and he convinced himself that Bob wanted to steal the church from him. He thought Bob was secretly planning to split the church. Nothing could have been further from the truth. Bob shares my conviction that church splits are a deep, fundamental violation of the very essence of biblical Christianity. I know Bob well enough to say with confidence that he would avoid being involved in a church split at all costs.

But once Tom got it in his mind that Bob wanted to steal church members, he read everything Bob did through that filter. He was sitting on the judgment seat misreading Bob's motives. Tom started talking negatively about Bob among the staff. There was a constant war behind the scenes in the church, which caused great damage within the congregation. Church members started leaving because, as they got wind of what was going on, they couldn't believe what was happening.

When Bob spoke with the pastor-friend who originally offered him the job at the church, the pastor suggested that Bob preach throughout the city, get a lot of people saved, and encourage them to follow him so that Tom would eventually feel he no longer belonged in the church and would resign. This was a warped plan that Bob refused to be part of.

Everything finally came to a head. The church's income had dropped so much they could no longer afford Bob's salary. One day Tom invited Bob into his office and told him he was being laid off. In an attempt to operate in the spirit of Christ, Bob offered to stay on staff salary-free. But Tom came clean and bluntly said, "I don't want you here anymore." Bob just loved on Tom, told him he respected his decision, and left his position at the church.

Three weeks later the senior pastor, Bob's friend in ministry, called the church board together to vote Tom out. He wanted to overthrow his friend! This pastor asked Bob and his family to attend the meeting. He said they could take back the church once Tom was gone and do "what God wanted us to do." Bob did not show up at the meeting.

Bob heard that the meeting turned into an ugly mess. People were screaming at one another, hurling accusations, cursing, and name-calling—all in a Sunday morning church service. Insecurity and inferiority, now fully displaying themselves, were empowered by people who were sitting on the judgment seat and assigning false motives to one another. This then gave each side of the dispute the justification they needed to act in a rebellious, ungodly manner.

False Discernment

It is unfortunate, but this has happened time and again in churches around the world. Insecurity and inferiority open the door for us to assign a false motive to someone's action, which then causes our perspective of what is real to change. Many times when Christians claim God has given them discernment about a situation, it is actually nothing more than a fear-based judgment of other people's motives that is rooted in the individuals' own insecurities and inferiorities.

I want you to let that sink deep inside your spirit. Say it out loud to yourself. *What many Christians call discernment is nothing more than a fear-based judgment of other people's motives that is rooted in their own insecurities and inferiorities.* We Christians assign spiritual language to justify feelings that are not based in reality. We love to say, "I sensed in my spirit," or "My spirit was grieved," or "I had a check in my spirit."

I know of a minister who dealt with this very situation several years ago. His church was in the midst of an incredible revival when one of his church members called him very disturbed. She said the Holy Spirit had been grieved and that she discerned during one of the revival services that there was division in the house. The pastor asked her to be more specific, but she just rambled using spiritual rhetoric. Finally the minister told the woman to stop with all the "spirit" talk, and he asked her point-blank, "What exactly are you talking about?"

It turned out that the woman thought this minister was angry with her. She struggled with fear of rejection, which is deeply rooted in insecurity and inferiority, and somehow the thought was planted in her mind that the pastor was upset with her. That thought then perverted her perception of everything that happened during the revival.

The woman thought the Holy Spirit had given her discernment about the revival. But her insecurities and inferiorities caused her to believe a lie that distorted her perspective. She assigned a false motive to her pastor—he was angry with her—that caused her to misjudge what God was doing at the revival.

The minister wasn't upset with the woman. He had no issue with her at all. The woman made a fear-based judgment about her pastor's feelings toward her, and that perverted her perception of everything that went on in the service. This woman had already started spreading her false perception to several other ladies, and a gossip circle began to spread a lie that a "spirit of division" was on some key leaders and that God was not pleased with the revival meetings. Fortunately the minister and this church member were able to talk things through and remove the lie before it did too much damage.

I believe this is the cause of most of the division people experience in relationships. They wrongly judge someone's motives because of their own insecurities and inferiorities. When this happens, fear gains a stronghold. Then the person becomes blind to the truth and incapable of properly seeing what is really going on behind the scenes.

This happens in marriages all the time. The enemy tells a wife her husband doesn't really value her. Then he reminds her of certain incidences to reinforce this thought. The devil says, "Look at how he doesn't help you with the dishes, or how he leaves his clothes on the floor, or how he didn't listen to you when he was watching the football game."

The wife begins to believe her husband does not value her.

She makes a false judgment rooted in insecurity and inferiority. Remember, inferiority is the sense or feeling of being lower in position, stature, or value. After listening to the enemy's lies, the wife begins to feel inferior. So she now has a filter in her mind that will distort her perception of everything her husband says or does.

He may tell her he loves her, but his words no longer make her feel the way they did back when they were dating. She begins to question whether he really means it when he tells her he loves her. She has made a fear-based judgment of his motives and now sees everything he does through that lens.

At this point fear has taken root in her—fear that her husband no longer loves her or values her the way he used to. She worries that he may start looking for somebody else. She becomes fearful that she will be trapped, misused, and maybe even abused in her marriage. This causes her to justify changing her attitude and behavior toward him. She starts griping and complaining. She becomes demanding and gets upset over the slightest things, maybe even accusing him of not caring or being there for her.

The couple may go to counseling now. She says he needs to do this and that to show that he values her. He makes efforts, but it never seems to be enough. Why? Because showing his wife how much he values her is only the symptom, not the problem. Until the wife discovers the root lie that caused her to question her husband's motives, she will keep finding a new complaint. There will be something else, then something else. After a while, the husband will get frustrated and may stop trying.

I could give you example after example of this taking place. I used this scenario of the wife who makes a false judgment about her husband's motives, but husbands do the same thing to their wives. Take the situation I described above. As the wife continually gripes and complains, the husband begins to feel emasculated. He believes his wife doesn't value or respect him, which makes him feel inferior and insecure. Now he too is wrongly judging his wife's motives.

He begins to react in order to protect himself. He starts to isolate himself, communicate less with his wife, and avoid being at home by burying himself in his work, hanging out with his guy friends, and the like. He now is reacting to her reaction to the lie the devil sowed in her mind. The husband's actions simply reinforce the wife's initial feeling that she was being devalued, and she becomes even more insecure and fearful and reacts more harshly to her husband when he is at home, which drives him even further away. The couple ends up in serious division, leading them to separate and consider divorce.

I've watched this happen over and over and over again, with various issues serving as the trigger. It could begin with a financial disagreement. He wants to spend a lot of money on a fancy gadget, new car, or snazzy media room. She's managing the checkbook and thinks they should save the money for a rainy day. He thinks she doesn't want him to have nice things. She thinks he doesn't care about the family's financial situation. They begin to fight because they wrongly judge each other's motive and think their spouse doesn't care or truly love them.

Or perhaps she is always running up credit card debt buying new dresses, shoes, and jewelry that she doesn't need. A fight ensues over how the money is being spent, and the couple becomes divided because of the financial pressure. She gains a feeling of security from having nice things, and he feels inferior because he is in debt. Although he is wise to want to become debt-free, both are getting their sense of value from something other than God. They are using money to gain a sense of worth, which we talked about in chapter 5.

This couple continues to assign false motives to each other, and they begin to fear what the other person will do to the family's finances. So they start separating their incomes and dividing every expense to the smallest detail. They're trying to protect themselves from their spouse's spending habits, but they're heading down a road that will lead only to further division.

We see the enemy use this divisive tactic among children most often when they enter their teen years. Satan is constantly using popular music, movies, video games, and television programs to sow lies in the younger generation that lead to mistrust. He tells them, "Your parents do not understand you. They do not care about you. They don't like who you have become, and they are only establishing these rules to keep you from doing what you want to do."

Once the enemy has convinced these youth to assign false motives to their parents and make wrong judgments as a result, the teenagers will feel justified in rejecting their parents' authority and doing whatever they want to do. These teens have fallen into the trap of the tree. They have partaken of the forbidden fruit and, like Adam and Eve, broken fellowship with God and the very source of life, which is Jesus Christ.

Judge Not

Before I venture deeper into this revelation, specifically how fear functions and what we can do to break its power off our lives, I want you to read this sentence to yourself out loud: *What many Christians call discernment is nothing more than a fear-based judgment of other people's motives that is rooted in their own insecurities and inferiorities.* We have to stop judging other people's motives—and God's—if we are ever going to walk in freedom from insecurity and inferiority. This is the sin I believe Jesus was dealing with in this passage in the Book of Matthew.

> Judge not, that you be not judged. For with what judgment you judge, you will be judged; and with the measure you use, it will be measured back to

you. And why do you look at the speck in your brother's eye, but do not consider the plank in your own eye? Or how can you say to your brother, "Let me remove the speck from your eye"; and look, a plank *is* in your own eye? Hypocrite! First remove the plank from your own eye, and then you will see clearly to remove the speck from your brother's eye.
—MATTHEW 7:1–5

Jesus said we are not to judge. What kind of judgment is He talking about, for the Bible says the spiritual man judges all things (1 Cor. 2:15)? A lot of people like to say, "Well, don't judge me" or "You're not supposed to judge me," when they're really just trying to keep you from challenging them to live holy before God. If you stand up and say certain things are sin, many people, especially in the media, will accuse you of judging. They'll say, "Jesus commands us not to judge." Even the heathen will try to use the Word to silence the preaching of righteousness.

That is not the judgment Jesus is talking about in Matthew 7. You are not judging people when you preach holy living. The Bible has already judged them. You are not being judgmental by simply declaring the Word of God.

The Bible says to not commit adultery, and we are to preach that around the world. The Bible says we are to forgive and to live holy. We are to flee the appearance of evil. The Bible says homosexual activity is a sin. It calls lying and cheating sins. It tells us to avoid immorality and says those engaged in those things will not enter the kingdom of heaven. To stand up and speak what the Bible says is not judging people. It is simply declaring what God has already said to be true. God is the One who has made the judgment about that issue.

So what is Jesus talking about in Matthew 7? He is not talking about applying the Word of God to people's actions and determining whether they line up. He is talking about making a judgment about people's motives. No one can truly know the motive of a person's heart except God. We can clearly say that someone is involved in a sinful act based on what the Word of God has declared is right or wrong. But we cannot say with certainty why people do what they do.

This is the trap we keep falling into. We keep wanting to assign motives to people's actions, but we don't really know. And because we keep assigning motives to people's actions, we often react by making choices that may not be named sins in the Bible but become sinful because they were done in the wrong spirit.

In Matthew 7, when Jesus cautioned us not to judge, He was telling us not to assign motives to people's actions, or the same thing will be done to us. I'm dealing with the issue of judging people's motives here. There is a place for true discernment, and I will discuss that in just a moment. The problem with assigning motives to people's actions is that as long as you are being influenced by insecurity and inferiority, you will not be able to see clearly. And if you can't see properly, your judgment will always be distorted. That is why Jesus tells us not to do that. It is not our job to go around judging people's hearts.

In Matthew 7:3, Jesus asked an important question we would be wise to ask ourselves. He said, "Why do you look at the speck in your brother's eye, but do not consider the plank in your own eye?" In other words, why are you trying to find the little hidden motive in your brother when you're not dealing with the huge plank of judging other people's motives because of the insecurity and inferiority hiding in your own heart?

Then He asks in the next verses, "Or how can you say to your brother, 'Let me remove the speck from your eye'; and look, a plank is in your own eye? Hypocrite! First remove the plank from your own eye, and then you will see clearly to remove the speck from your brother's eye." Look at that. Jesus said only after you get the plank out of your eye will you be able to see properly so you can help your brother. As long as you are being driven by insecurity and inferiority, you cannot correctly discern what is going on in somebody else's life. The insecurity and inferiority in your heart will cause you to wrongly judge other people's motives, which will distort your perspective of everything.

You may be wondering how you can know the difference between judgment and discerning what is going on in someone's life. Here is one way. If your supposed discernment produces in you feelings of hurt, woundedness, or fear, or a desire for self-protection or self-preservation, then you are operating out of selfishness and not love. Only through agape love can you properly see, properly discern, and properly deal with situations in other people's lives. And as long as your reactions are about self, you are not operating in agape love. You are operating out of your own insecurities and inferiorities. Take a step back and see if the conflicts you are having in your relationships are due to the fact that you have judged someone else's motives. Be honest with yourself. If you have, repent for sitting on the judgment seat. Ask God to cleanse you of any false perceptions you may have developed so you can see that person as He does. As you start examining yourself, you will likely be shocked by how many people you have wrongly judged. Ask God to fill you with the love of Christ for those people, no matter what they have done.

In order to truly get victory over insecurity and inferiority, we have to break through the two great walls that surround these two demon spirits. These walls keep us from truly dealing with the root issues and getting free. The first is the one we just addressed—assigning motives to people's actions, as if we can judge their hearts. The second wall is the one Satan uses to fortify the spirits of insecurity and inferiority. It has a very familiar name: fear.

13

WALLS OF FEAR

*For God has not given us a spirit of fear, but of
power and of love and of a sound mind.*
—2 TIMOTHY 1:7

WHEN WE BEGIN to understand how we assign false
motives to people's actions and use the judgments
we make about them to justify our wrong behavior,
we can start moving down a path that leads to true freedom
from insecurity and inferiority. But we still face one other
major enemy that works to keep us from getting deep enough
below the surface to lay the ax at the root of these two demonic
spirits.

This enemy attacks, torments, and influences probably nine
out of ten Christians. It operates by building a wall so fortified
that it inhibits the truth from penetrating deep enough for the
person to truly break free from the grip of insecurity and inferiority. The enemy I am talking about is the spirit of fear.

In the last chapter I told you about the source of some
Christians' discernment. This is an important concept for you
to understand. *What most Christians call discernment is nothing
more than a fear-based judgment of other people's motives that is
rooted in their own insecurities and inferiorities.* This judgment of
other people's motives is based in fear. In order to better understand how Satan uses fear to fortify the spirits of insecurity and
inferiority, we must again go back to the Garden of Eden.

> And they heard the sound of the LORD God
> walking in the garden in the cool of the day,
> and Adam and his wife hid themselves from the
> presence of the LORD God among the trees of the
> garden. Then the LORD God called to Adam and
> said to him, "Where are you?" So he said, "I heard
> Your voice in the garden, and I was afraid because
> I was naked; and I hid myself."
>
> —GENESIS 3:8–10

After Adam and Eve sinned and realized they were naked, they heard the sound of the Lord God walking in the garden, and they immediately reacted in fear. Instead of rushing to Him as they used to, they hid themselves from the presence of the Lord among the trees. Adam and Eve's actions reveal an important truth that we must grab hold of—*fear will cause you to withdraw from the presence of God.*

Adam told God he was afraid because he was now exposed, and he hid himself from God as a result. Adam and Eve had always been physically naked, but the presence of God revealed their spiritual condition. They were sinners with nowhere to hide from a holy God. When Adam and Eve started to see their true spiritual state, fear gripped their hearts. Fear always brings with it feelings of judgment and loss, and fear represents the opposite of who God is. First John 4:18 says, "There is no fear in love; but perfect love casts out fear, because fear involves torment. But he who fears has not been made perfect in love."

Fear becomes a stronghold in our lives because it is rooted in our desire to protect ourselves from some potential judgment, punishment, pain, or suffering. Fear will cause us to hide. It will cause us to deny the truth. It will cause us to flee the very presence of God. Fear will rob us of our destiny, and it must not be tolerated in any way. It must be destroyed.

Fear attaches itself so easily to the person who is operating under the influence of insecurity and inferiority. These two demon spirits give fear access to our lives and empower fear to torment us. Fear then works to protect these two demon spirits from being exposed and ultimately cast out.

Second Timothy 1:7 says, "For God has not given us a spirit of fear, but of power and of love and of a sound mind." God has not given us a spirit of fear, nor does He want us to operate under any influence of fear. Fear blinds us from the truth. It drives us in a direction completely opposite from where God is. We must get a revelation of the seriousness, the danger, and the sinfulness of allowing fear to operate in any area of our life. There is no way you will truly get free from Satan's dirty little secret—the spirits of insecurity and inferiority—until you break the barricade of fear insulating those two strongholds.

In order to break through this barricade of fear, we have to attack it from two fronts. First, we must recognize fear for what it is—a sin that God has clearly commanded us to resist. And second, we must get to know the weapons God has given us to break the power of fear over our lives.

God has promised that we can truly be free of fear, but we're going to have to repent of this sin. You might say, "Pastor Steve, it's a little harsh to call fear sin." But recognizing fear as sin is the first step toward breakthrough. We just read in 2 Timothy 1:7 that God has not given us a spirit of fear. This is just one of many warnings God gives us against fear.

The Bible says in Revelation 21:8 that "the fearful, and unbelieving, and the abominable, and murderers, and whoremongers, and sorcerers, and idolaters, and all liars, shall have their part in the lake which burneth with fire and brimstone: which is the second death" (kjv). God said the lake of fire is reserved for murderers, sorcerers, all liars, idolaters, and whoremongers, but the first group on that list is the fearful. The word *fearful* here means cowardly.[1] It is the same word used in Matthew 8:26 when Jesus spoke to the winds and waves, and calmed the storm. He said to His disciples, "Why are you fearful, O you of little faith?" The lake of fire is reserved not only for those who cower in the face of persecution but also for those who shrink away from radical obedience to God because of fear.

Repeatedly throughout Scripture, God commanded His people not to fear.

> And the LORD, He *is* the One who goes before you. He will be with you, He will not leave you nor forsake you; do not fear nor be dismayed.
> —DEUTERONOMY 31:8

> Have I not commanded you? Be strong and of good courage; do not be afraid, nor be dismayed, for the LORD your God is with you wherever you go.
> —JOSHUA 1:9

> "Do not be afraid of their faces, for I *am* with you to deliver you," says the LORD.
> —JEREMIAH 1:8

When God addressed the issue of fear, He commanded His people to not be afraid. This is not just a word of encouragement or a suggestion from the Almighty. It is an absolute command to flee from, avoid, and resist this demonic spirit called fear.

So why is God so adamantly against fear? Why has He commanded us to flee from it, and why did He reserve such horrific judgment for those who are being controlled by this spirit? To answer these questions, we must look at the very nature of fear itself.

A SELF-IMPOSED PRISON

Fear operates by getting people to put their attention on themselves. It causes a person to focus on self-preservation and to reject anything that threatens his or her self-interest. This is completely contrary to the entire message of the gospel.

> Then He said to them all, "If anyone desires to
> come after Me, let him deny himself, and take up
> his cross daily, and follow Me. For whoever desires
> to save his life will lose it, but whoever loses his
> life for My sake will save it. For what profit is it to
> a man if he gains the whole world, and is himself
> destroyed or lost? For whoever is ashamed of Me
> and My words, of him the Son of Man will be
> ashamed when He comes in His own glory, and in
> His Father's, and of the holy angels."
>
> —LUKE 9:23–26

The gospel is about self-denial while the essence of fear is self-preservation. Jesus told us to take up our crosses and follow Him (Luke 9:23), but fear tells to us do what is in our best interest. Fear is a powerful demonic spirit because it gets us so focused on self-preservation that we stop thinking practically and rationally; instead we begin operating from a state of complete carnality. When we operate in fear, we think solely about ourselves.

Because fear is all about self-preservation, it causes us to hide and push away anything we perceive as a threat. We become so determined to protect ourselves that we build walls of defense. These walls affect our relationships with the people around us and with God. And they become the filter through which we perceive everything.

In the last chapter we looked at how judging people based on false assumptions about their motives keeps us from seeing clearly. Fear makes us so self-focused that we end up in a position where we cannot clearly see the truth. This is because God cannot be separated from truth, and God is love. Therefore all truth must function from love, and anything not done through the filter of love cannot accurately present the truth.

We build these walls of defense thinking they will protect us, but they don't actually work to keep bad things from happening. Instead they rob us of fellowship with God and other believers by causing us to withdraw, and they block the plan, purpose, and will of God for our lives. In the end, the walls we build out of fear to protect ourselves become a prison that ensnares us. I pray you will let that truth get deep inside your spirit—*the walls you build out of fear to protect yourself will become the very prison that ensnares you.*

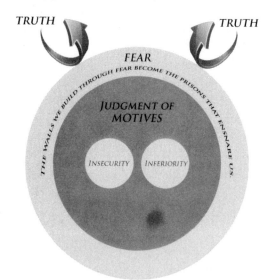

Fear lies to us. It tells us that if we submit to it, we will be safe. But fear's intention is actually to enslave us and keep us contained inside its walls. As you are reading these words, I know you are feeling a quickening in your spirit. The Holy Spirit is pointing out areas in your life and in your relationships where you are functioning in fear, places where you have built walls in an attempt to protect yourself, only to find that those walls have become your very prison.

I have seen this happen so often in people's lives. At The Upper Room Church, where I am the senior pastor, I have seen these walls in many of the people who have come into our church. Some of the people went through horrific personal tragedies, abuses, and failures; others experienced great disappointments, hurts, and wounds in previous churches.

They would come into our church and love the worship, embrace the powerful revelation from God's Word, and be thrilled to see the Holy Spirit moving so freely among us. But they would always have up a wall. They were always just a bit skeptical about what God was doing at The Upper Room Church, so they would hesitate to fully jump into the move of God. Fear would be telling them, "Don't trust Pastor Steve. Preachers have hurt you before. You've heard the good talk before. Don't trust because that will make you too vulnerable, and you will be hurt again."

The problem is, the only way they could fully receive of the powerful move of the Holy Spirit our church was experiencing was if they opened their heart, submitted to the leadership, followed the leading of the Holy Spirit, and surrendered themselves completely to God. I watched so many people hang out on the edge of the move of God but not dive in because they kept listening to fear.

Many of these people would attend our church for months and receive a powerful touch from the Lord. I would spend time with them and love on them. I would open up my life and my home in order to show them the reality of my commitment to Christ. I am determined to live out the gospel in private as well as in public. These fear-bound church members could see the integrity and the honesty in my lifestyle, and I often heard them make comments about how wonderful it was to be in a church where the leadership was so transparent and so passionate about living holy before God.

But then fear would start talking to them again. If I used one phrase a former pastor used or made one gesture that reminded them of something that happened in a previous church, fear would blow it up and make it seem like a huge threat. The next thing I knew those members would be sending me letters explaining that they were leaving the church because they felt they couldn't trust me. They would say I had rejected them or didn't appreciate what they had to offer.

Insecurity and inferiority were screaming at them, so these precious people would withdraw into their protective walls, thinking they would be safe. But the walls they built out of fear cut them off from what God wanted to do in their lives through the church and the God-ordained relationships they had formed there. Those walls were doing exactly what fear wanted them to—causing these dear people to live in a prison of their own making.

I often spent hours counseling these people and talking them through the lies that flooded their minds in order to bring them back to truth and reality. Most of the time the individuals would see what I was talking about, repent, and get involved in the work of God again. But if the person didn't deal with the root of fear, it would rear its ugly head again within a few months. The person would experience something new that made him feel rejected or unsafe, and he would again withdraw into the prison walls of his own fears.

THE OPPOSITE OF FAITH

I have found that fear has robbed more Christians of their ministry potential than any immorality has ever done. I am a strong holiness preacher. Yet as rampant as immorality is, I don't believe it has done as much damage within the church as the sin of fear.

The sin of fear is what caused Peter to deny Jesus (Mark 14:66–72). The sin of fear is what caused John Mark to flee on the missionary journey with the apostle Paul (Acts 13:13; 15:36–41). The sin of fear is what caused David to sin against God by taking a census of Israel before the battle (1 Chron. 21:1–7). The sin of fear is what caused Abraham to lie and say that his wife was really his sister, putting her in danger of being violated by the leader of Egypt (Gen. 12:10–20).

The sin of fear causes God's people to be reserved in worship, withhold their tithes and offerings, reject God's spiritual authority by dishonoring His established leadership in the church, break off relationships, get divorced, fail to evangelize, and refuse to boldly stand for the gospel of Jesus Christ. The sin of fear keeps people from praying for the sick, from casting out devils, and from standing for righteousness in a world so bent on wickedness.

The sin of fear has caused so many pastors to compromise the preaching of the gospel in order to keep a large crowd. They refuse to use the word *repentance* and won't demand that people turn from the wickedness of their sin because they believe the lie that our society today will not accept such a strong message. These ministry leaders are so bound by the fear of man, which is rooted in their desire to gain their sense of value and identity through the size of their congregation, that they ultimately reject the message Jesus sent them to preach. They compromise God's standards of holiness, belittle the call to separate from the world, fail to teach the paths of righteousness, and try to create an atmosphere in the church that is so comfortable for sinners it is devoid of any real power to convict.

This is not what God wants for His church. "God has not given us a spirit of fear, but of power and of love and of a sound mind" (2 Tim. 1:7). Fear is our greatest enemy. It is an enemy that can literally strip away our relationship with God. We must view it as something that must be destroyed in our lives.

In order to defeat fear, we must understand its nature and the weapons God has given us to fight it. I am sure you have heard preachers say fear is the opposite of faith. I want to challenge that teaching. Fear is not the opposite of faith. Doubt is the opposite of faith. We can see this revelation in the account of Jesus walking on the water.

> Now in the fourth watch of the night Jesus went to
> them, walking on the sea. And when the disciples
> saw Him walking on the sea, they were troubled,
> saying, "It is a ghost!" And they cried out for fear.
> But immediately Jesus spoke to them, saying, "Be
> of good cheer! It is I; do not be afraid."
>
> —MATTHEW 14:25–27

In this story we see all three elements at work. We see fear, we see doubt, and we see Jesus comment on faith. When the disciples saw Jesus walking on the water, they cried out in fear. Jesus spoke and told them to be of good cheer. The phrase *good cheer* literally means "have courage."[2] Jesus said, "It is I; do not be afraid." Peter, emboldened by Jesus's word, then said:

> "Lord, if it is You, command me to come to You on
> the water." So He said, "Come." And when Peter
> had come down out of the boat, he walked on the
> water to go to Jesus. But when he saw that the
> wind was boisterous, he was afraid; and beginning
> to sink he cried out, saying, "Lord, save me!" And
> immediately Jesus stretched out His hand and
> caught him, and said to him, "O you of little faith,
> why did you doubt?" And when they got into the
> boat, the wind ceased.
>
> —MATTHEW 14:28–32

Peter got out of the boat, but then he saw that the situation was dangerous. He became afraid and started to sink. This is where people get confused about the difference between faith, doubt, and fear. They think the fear was the opposite reaction to the faith Peter should have had in Jesus when He commanded him to come. Peter's fear, however, was the result of doubt.

Jesus responded to Peter by saying, "O you of little faith, why did you doubt?" He didn't say, "O you of little faith, why did you fear?" Jesus said, "Why did you doubt?" because doubt is the opposite of faith. When Peter began to doubt the safety, security, and lasting effect of Jesus's command, he looked at his circumstances and thought his life was in danger. That is when fear entered in. When Peter doubted the Word of God and stopped trusting in Jesus's ability to preserve him, he became filled with fear.

Fear is all about self-preservation. I hope you will get that deep inside your spirit. Because fear is all about self-preservation, God commands us not to fear. The very nature of fear is completely opposite to the very nature of God.

As we saw earlier, "There is no fear in love; but perfect love casts out fear, because fear involves torment. But he who fears has not been made perfect in love" (1 John 4:18). Fear and love cannot coexist. In this verse John is saying that no fear exists in agape love. The very nature of love literally drives fear out. He explains this by saying fear involves torment.

The person who fears is focused on himself. Agape love is all about self-denial. Agape love is not an emotion. It is a choice. Agape love is a deliberate act of the will to do what is in the best interest of another, regardless of the personal consequences. Fear, on the other hand, will keep a person inwardly focused and blind him to the things of God. Let's look again at the story in Matthew.

> Now in the fourth watch of the night Jesus went to them, walking on the sea. And when the disciples saw Him walking on the sea, they were troubled, saying, "It is a ghost!" And they cried out for fear. But immediately Jesus spoke to them, saying, "Be of good cheer! It is I; do not be afraid."
> —MATTHEW 14:25–27

Here comes Jesus walking on the water. Why didn't the disciples recognize Him? They had just been with Him and saw amazing miracles take place. Why did they now think He was a ghost? Fear blinded them from recognizing Jesus, so they couldn't see who was coming to them. This is exactly what happens to many of us when Jesus comes to deal with an area of our lives that makes us feel insecure or inferior.

Fear will keep you from seeing that it is Jesus coming to you. This is why I said we have to deal with fear before we can destroy the power of insecurity and inferiority in our lives. Jesus had to first deal with the root of fear when He ministered to His anxious disciples in Matthew 14. He said, "Be of good cheer! It is I; do not be afraid" (v. 27).

Jesus was saying, "Take courage! It is I." This is the same thing He is about to say to you in the next few chapters: "Take courage! It is I. Don't be afraid of Me coming to you in the night—in the dark places of your heart. I want to come and bring peace to the turmoil in your innermost being. *Be not afraid.*"

Jesus gave us a most amazing weapon against fear, and that is agape love. This love is supernatural. It is given by the Holy Spirit, and it is the element that changed everything for the disciples. Only agape love has the ability to cast out fear and bring you into true freedom. The walls of fear we have built in an attempt to protect ourselves must be destroyed, and this will only happen if we truly get a revelation of the power of agape love.

14

THE POWER OF AGAPE LOVE

There is no fear in love; but perfect love casts out fear.
—I JOHN 4:18

As we learned in the last chapter, fear will form a barrier in our lives that hinders us from hearing the truth of God's Word and allowing it to break through to the deepest parts of our heart and free us from our insecurities and inferiorities. If we allow it to have free rein, fear will cause us to withdraw from God and our commitment to Him. And because it keeps us from seeing the power of truth, it will lead us into disobedience.

But God has given us a weapon. First John 4:18 tells us that agape love destroys fear. In this chapter we will examine the amazing weapon God gave us to conquer fear by looking at the greatest failure of a man Jesus had previously heralded for his great faith. Peter walked on water, and Jesus called him the "rock" upon which He would build His church. But even this disciple fell prey to the spirit of fear when he made the devastating decision to deny Jesus—not once but three times.

Peter committed this incredible failure out of a desire to protect himself. Through every step of Peter's denial, from the Garden of Gethsemane to the temple, we see insecurity and inferiority at work behind the wall of fear. This story also reveals the amazing way Jesus exposed Peter's problem and led him to true freedom. But first, let's go back to the events that led up to Jesus's arrest and allow truth to break through into our lives.

> Then Jesus said to them, "All of you will be made to stumble because of Me this night, for it is written: 'I will strike the Shepherd, and the sheep of the flock will be scattered.' But after I have been raised, I will go before you to Galilee." Peter answered and said to Him, *"Even if all are made to stumble because of You, I will never be made to stumble."* Jesus said to him, *"Assuredly, I say to you that this night, before the rooster crows, you will deny Me three times."* Peter said to Him, *"Even if I have to die with You, I will not deny You!"* And so said all the disciples.
>
> —MATTHEW 26:31–35, EMPHASIS ADDED

You will often find that the people who make the most grandiose claims are the ones who wrestle the most with insecurity and inferiority. Peter was adamant that he would not deny Christ. He was so sure that he was stronger than all the rest. The truth is, Peter used his brash and boastful personality to hide his fears and insecurities. Peter's pride was masking his fear.

Fear didn't just sneak up on him. Peter always had a fear problem that kept the truth of Jesus's words from breaking through. Think about it. Peter watched as Jesus fulfilled prophecy after prophecy. He saw Jesus heal the sick, cast out demons, and feed thousands of people with two fish and five loaves of bread. Peter knew Jesus's track record. Yet when Jesus told Peter that he would deny Him three times, Peter argued back and said, "Even if I have to die with You, I will not deny You!"

The truth Jesus spoke couldn't break through because of the wall of fear Peter built around his heart. God knew this about Peter, which is why He allowed him to experience such an embarrassing sifting. When big, brawny Peter was confronted by a servant girl in the courtyard of the high priest, he cowered in fear. He was so intimidated by the girl's accusation that he was one of Jesus's disciples that Peter denied the Lord—just a few hours after he proclaimed that he would never do any such thing. And before the night was over, Peter denied Jesus two more times.

> Now Peter sat outside in the courtyard. And a servant girl came to him, saying, "You also were with Jesus of Galilee." But he denied it before them all, saying, "I do not know what you are saying." And when he had gone out to the gateway, another girl saw him and said to those who were there, "This fellow also was with Jesus of Nazareth." But again he denied with an oath, "I do not know the Man!" And a little later those who stood by came up and said to Peter, "Surely you also are one of them, for your speech betrays you." Then he began to curse and swear, saying, "I do not know the Man!" Immediately a rooster crowed. And Peter remembered the word of Jesus who had said to him, "Before the rooster crows, you will deny Me three times." So he went out and wept bitterly.
>
> —MATTHEW 26:69–75

The manifestation of Peter's fear was so strong he even began to curse. Suddenly Peter was utterly exposed. He was now laid bare before all. Peter probably didn't feel like much of a rock at that point. But after Christ's resurrection, Jesus approached Peter and initiated the following exchange, which many preachers call "the restoration of Peter":

> So when they had eaten breakfast, Jesus said to Simon Peter, "Simon, son of Jonah, do you love Me more than these?" He said to Him, "Yes, Lord;

> You know that I love You." He said to him, "Feed
> My lambs." He said to him again a second time,
> "Simon, son of Jonah, do you love Me?" He said
> to Him, "Yes, Lord; You know that I love You."
> He said to him, "Tend My sheep." He said to him
> the third time, "Simon, son of Jonah, do you love
> Me?" Peter was grieved because He said to him the
> third time, "Do you love Me?" And he said to Him,
> "Lord, You know all things; You know that I love
> You." Jesus said to him, "Feed My sheep.
>
> —John 21:15–17

Many ministers claim that because Peter denied the Lord three times, Jesus asked him three times if he loved Him in order to reconcile Peter to Himself and renew his commission to ministry. We are about to discover this is *not* what happened. This discourse was *not* Jesus's way of restoring Peter but of fully exposing what Peter still lacked. In order to understand what really transpired here we must look into the meaning of the Greek words used in this passage.

> Jesus said to Simon Peter, "Simon, son of Jonah, do
> you love Me more than these?" He said to Him,
> "Yes, Lord; You know that I love You." He said to
> him, "Feed My lambs."
>
> —John 21:15

The word *love* in Jesus's question in this verse is the Greek word *agapao*, which comes from the root word *agape*. Agape is a supernatural love. It is God's love.[1] This is important to note because Peter responds to Jesus by saying, "Yes, Lord; You know that I love You." But Peter didn't say he *agape* loved Jesus, he said he *phileo* loved Jesus. *Phileo* is another Greek word for love, but it refers to brotherly love or a deep human emotion of affection for someone else.[2] Jesus asked Peter, "Do you have God's love for Me?" And Peter replied by saying, "I have brotherly love for You."

Jesus then asked Peter a second time, "Simon, son of Jonah, do you love [*agape*] Me?" And Peter answered again by saying, "Yes, Lord; You know that I love [*phileo*] You." Twice now Jesus has asked Peter if he *agape* loved Him, and twice Peter answered by saying he had *phileo* love for Him. Then Jesus drove the truth home with His third question.

Jesus said to Peter the third time, "Simon, son of Jonah, do you love [*phileo*] Me?" The third time Jesus changed the question. He lowered the standard from God's agape love to mere human *phileo* love, thus exposing what Peter was lacking. Peter became grieved because he now fully understood what Jesus was asking, and he knew he was fully exposed.

John 21:17 says, "Peter was grieved because He said to him *the third time*, 'Do you love [*phileo*] Me?' And he said to Him, 'Lord, You know all things; You know that I love [*phileo*] You.'" Peter was saying, "Lord, You know I do not have agape love. I have only human, brotherly affection for You."

AN IMMERSION OF AGAPE

The agape love of God cannot be faked. It is a supernatural love. It is *not* an emotion. Jesus said, "Greater love has no one than this, than to lay down one's life for his friends" (John 15:13). What Jesus was exposing to Peter was that he lacked the one key element he needed to truly fulfill his destiny.

Peter walked with Jesus. He talked with Jesus. He saw the miracles Jesus performed. He heard His amazing teaching. Peter also walked in miracles himself. Yet all of these things were not enough to keep Peter from denying the Lord. All of these experiences—all the words he heard preached and all the supernatural signs he witnessed—still couldn't break through the fear barriers in his life and annihilate the roots of insecurity and inferiority.

After Jesus exposed what Peter was lacking, He told Peter there was something he needed. Jesus commanded Peter to wait in Jerusalem for the Father to send what He promised. He and the rest of the early disciples were to await a supernatural encounter with the Holy Spirit. Jesus knew this experience would give Peter what he was lacking and allow him to become the mighty man of God that God always intended him to be.

Peter didn't understand all of this. He knew only what Jesus said immediately before He ascended into heaven: "But you shall receive power when the Holy Spirit has come upon you; and you shall be witnesses to Me in Jerusalem, and in all Judea and Samaria, and to the end of the earth" (Acts 1:8).

Jesus wanted the disciples to wait in Jerusalem until they received what we call the baptism of the Holy Spirit. He said that they would receive power—a supernatural power that would enable them to be His witnesses. Unfortunately, in many parts of the Spirit-filled community we have taught predominantly about the manifestation of speaking in tongues as the evidence that a person has received the baptism of the Holy Spirit.

Although tongues is an amazing supernatural gift, it is not the primary evidence Jesus wanted His followers to display. In Acts 1:8 Jesus said the disciples would receive supernatural, miracle-working power when the Holy Spirit came upon them, and that power would enable them to be His witnesses. The word *witness* there comes from the Greek word *martus*, which is also translated "martyr."[3] A martyr is one who has laid his life down for a cause.

In this verse Jesus was telling the disciples and Peter that they needed to wait until they received a supernatural saturation of the power of His Spirit that would give them the ability to lay down their lives for the sake of the gospel. They were to be baptized, or completely immersed, in the Holy Spirit.

The Bible declares that God is love. We also understand that the Holy Spirit is fully God. Therefore, the Holy Spirit is also love. The Holy Spirit is agape. So if a person is baptized (completely immersed) in the Holy Spirit, then he is baptized, or completely immersed, in agape. Jesus exposed Peter's problem as a lack of agape love. He told Peter to go to Jerusalem and wait to receive this most incredible supernatural experience that would indue him with agape love.

The true baptism of the Holy Spirit is about being immersed in the agape love of God. Romans 5:5 says, "Now hope does not disappoint, because the love of God has been poured out in our hearts by the Holy Spirit who was given to us." Paul declares that the love of God has been poured out in our hearts by the Holy Spirit. This pouring out of the agape love of God is the key to us having the power to die to ourselves. It is this agape love that is the weapon God has given us to break through the fear barriers in our lives in order that truth can penetrate and finally deliver us from the bondages of insecurity and inferiority. The illustration below shows this process at work.

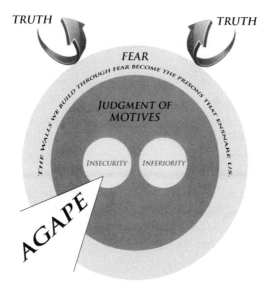

Perfect agape casts out fear. It is the agape love of God that breaks through the fear barrier. This makes sense if you think about it. Fear is all about self-preservation; agape love is all about self-denial. The self-denying power of agape love casts out all the self-preserving strongholds built by fear.

Once Peter got a hold of this breakthrough, we don't see him denying the Lord anymore. On the Day of Pentecost he stood up in front of the same kind of crowd he cowered to before and boldly declared the gospel of Jesus Christ (Acts 2:14–47). In order for us to reach the place where truth can penetrate our hearts and deliver us from the power of insecurity and inferiority, we must experience the agape love of God that tears down the walls of fear.

It is not enough to simply quote scriptures about the love of God, believe in the love of God, or even confess that you are loved by God. You must have an experience with the supernatural agape love of God. The apostle Paul made this one of the cornerstones of his teachings in the epistles. In his letter to the Ephesians, Paul prayed that they would know the agape love of God:

> May you be rooted deep in love and founded securely on love, that you may have the power and be strong to apprehend and grasp with all the saints [God's devoted people, the experience of that love] what is the breadth and length and height and depth [of it]; [that you may really come] to know [practically, through experience for yourselves] the love of Christ, which far surpasses mere knowledge [without experience]; that you may be filled [through all your being] unto all the fullness of God [may have the richest measure of the divine Presence, and become a body wholly filled and flooded with God Himself]!
>
> —EPHESIANS 3:17–19, AMP

Paul's prayer here is that you may come to know the agape love of God through an experience with His agape love. He says that after this experience with the agape love of God, you will then become filled with the fullness of God. We need that in the body of Christ today. We need a fresh release of the agape love of God and to be filled with the fullness of God. This needs to become our heart cry and earnest prayer. We need to boldly come before God and plead, "Lord, baptize us in Your agape love."

When we receive these experiences of the agape love of God and as we act in agape love, it will grow more and more in our lives. Whatever we release will increase. So the more we choose to deny ourselves and walk in agape love, the more God will release greater measures of His love in our lives.

It is fear that keeps us from receiving the revelation truths we need to truly walk free from the spirits of insecurity and inferiority. But God has given us a supernatural weapon to destroy its power. That weapon is the agape love of God.

I pray right now by the power of the Holy Spirit that God will release into your life new encounters and new experiences with His agape love. I pray these experiences will overwhelm you, that you will know the height and depth and length and breadth of the love of God, and that you will experience the fullness of His love.

By faith right now, lift your hands wherever you are reading this book and ask God to give you a new experience with His agape love. Ask Him to just flood your heart with this amazing, powerful love. This is a vital step to begin the process of truly breaking free from the spirits of insecurity and inferiority. When the fear barriers start to come down, you will then be positioned to receive of the spirit of wisdom and revelation. This is what will finally crush the power of insecurity and inferiority over your life.

15
THE SPIRIT OF WISDOM AND REVELATION

But we all, with unveiled face, beholding as in a mirror the glory of the Lord, are being transformed into the same image from glory to glory, just as by the Spirit of the Lord.
—2 CORINTHIANS 3:18

ONE OF THE most transforming events of my life took place in February 1987. I had been saved only a few months when inside of me arose a deep desire to pray for the ability to work the works of God supernaturally. A spirit of prayer came upon me for weeks.

I had been radically saved May 2, 1986, and instantly delivered from five years of drug addiction. Not only did God deliver me from the addiction, but He also forever removed the desire from me. Two days after I was saved, God spoke to me while I was on my knees worshiping and said, "I have called you to preach My gospel." He showed me in a vision all the plans and dreams I had for my life. When I responded, "Yes, Lord, I will," I saw my plans fade off in the distance, and then God gloriously baptized me in the Holy Spirit.

It didn't take long for me to realize that the church was lacking the one element that was key to my deliverance. I knew this key was desperately needed to deliver my generation. It was the supernatural power of God. Although the ministry I was saved under moved in the power, I knew of many churches that didn't, and I saw the negative results of that. I saw a lethargy and weakness within those congregations. I saw people going to church but having no victory in life.

By the time the year was drawing to a close, I had been praying for weeks that God would anoint me to minister with power. As December 1986 came upon me, a deep cry rose up from within me. I prayed, "God, I must have the power to reach my generation!" I began to pray more than four hours a day. I was focused on one thing: "God, give to me the power."

As the New Year rolled around, a friend of mine told me about a mighty man of God by the name of Morris Cerullo. He told me that he had never seen anybody move in such power. He talked about a world conference that Morris Cerullo held at the beginning of each year. My friend told me about how the glory of God would fill the whole hotel and how people would be caught away into Spirit in their hotel rooms.

I was so intrigued that I asked my friend if I could borrow a tape series by Dr. Cerullo called *Proof Producers*. My friend was hesitant to lend the tapes because he was afraid he would never get them back. Those of you who have "loaned" books and tapes will relate to his concern. After much begging on my part, he loaned them to me. I drove back home to San Diego, and on Thursday morning of the first week of January 1987 I sat down in front of my tape deck with my Bible opened ready to hear a good message.

As Dr. Cerullo began to preach, I thought his voice was really raspy and the organ irritating. Then he said for us to look at our hands. He said, "The future success of the work of God lies in the hands of those who can answer this question: 'What must we do that we might work the works of God?'"[1]

I was hooked. My Bible dropped to the floor as a wave of the Holy Spirit hit the crowd on the tape. That same wave hit me in my home. I began to cry out to God, "I must have the power!" For the next three hours I listened to Dr. Cerullo preach as wave after wave of the Holy Spirit would hit, then

Dr. Cerullo would continue to preach. With tears in my eyes I cried out, "This is it! This is it!" I knew in my heart of hearts this man had the anointing I needed.

I finished the first three hours of the tapes and then went into my room to pray for an hour. I came out after prayer to listen to more of the tapes. I was putting the next tape in the cassette player when God spoke to me and said, "Pack your bags and go to the World Conference." I didn't know where the conference was, so I looked on the tape and saw an address, called information to get the number, and spoke with someone from the ministry five minutes before their offices closed.

The ministry representative told me the conference started the previous Tuesday and was being held at the Hilton Hotel next to Disneyland in Southern California, which was about a two-hour drive away. I grabbed a grocery bag, threw in some clothes, wrote a note to my roommate, and left for the conference with only fifty dollars to my name.

When I arrived at the conference, Dr. Cerullo was already preaching. I sat in an overflow room and watched him on a giant screen. Just like on the tapes, waves of the Holy Spirit would sweep the room. I was overwhelmed by the manifested presence of God as Dr. Cerullo preached on the glory of God, the *doxa*.

A final wave of the Spirit hit the meeting. I was standing and crying out to God when I felt a giant hand from heaven come and touch my head. Immediately I fell to the ground, overpowered by the presence of God. I lay there for quite a while. When I got up, I told some other conference attendees about my day. They immediately opened their hotel room to me. I was ready to fast throughout the conference and sleep in my car because this was my breakthrough, but the Lord had another plan.

I could hardly sleep that night. I was up at six thirty the next morning to go down to the meeting room for prayer. I was in the main hall from 6:30 a.m. till 5:30 p.m. I didn't want to miss a thing. Somehow I ended up on the front row for the evening service, and Jesus preached to us through Dr. Cerullo for three hours. Yes, it might have been Morris Cerullo holding the microphone, but it was Jesus who preached to us about His agape love. I sat there with my jaw to the floor, knowing that this man carried the anointing that could change a world.

OPENING THE EYES OF OUR HEARTS

That night God led me to become a ministry partner and learn at the feet of His servant. A few weeks after I became a partner, the ministry sent me Dr. Cerullo's complete teaching series from the conference, which was titled *Unity in the Spirit*. While listening to the tapes, I saw a vision and received an anointing that forever changed my life and continues to change it today.

There was a section on the tapes where Dr. Cerullo preached from Ephesians 1:17–19. He spent seven to ten minutes talking about the passage. As Dr. Cerullo preached, something inside me was so deeply stirred that I had to listen to that segment over and over again. Each time I listened to it, the presence of God would come on me. I knew there was something deeper there than I was seeing at first. So I listened over and over and prayed.

After about two hours of this my roommate came home. I tried to tell him what I was experiencing, but every time I began to speak, I would become overwhelmed and start crying. Three times I tried to tell him, and the third time it happened. As I tried to explain what I was experiencing, I saw a full-blown open vision. It was so overwhelming I dropped to the ground and cried out, "I see it! I see it!"

What did I see? That the God of our Lord Jesus Christ, the Father of glory, wants to give us the spirit of wisdom and revelation in the knowledge of Him (Eph. 1:17). The Amplified

Bible says it this way: "[For I always pray to] the God of our Lord Jesus Christ, the Father of glory, that He may grant you a spirit of wisdom and revelation [of insight into mysteries and secrets] in the [deep and intimate] knowledge of Him."

This was not just the prayer of the apostle Paul. It was the prayer of the Holy Spirit, because all Scripture is given by inspiration of God (2 Tim. 3:16). The Holy Spirit told Paul what to pray. The Bible tells us in 2 Peter 1:20–21 that "no prophecy of Scripture is of any private interpretation, for prophecy never came by the will of man, but holy men of God spoke as they were moved by the Holy Spirit." This prayer in Ephesians 1 was from God for the most spiritual people of Paul's day. This was not for the baby Christians. The church at Ephesus was the most mature group, and the Book of Ephesians gives the deepest look at the purpose for the existence of the church.

It is to these people that Paul prays the prayer of the Holy Spirit that God would give them a spirit of wisdom and revelation. Now there is only one Holy Spirit, so what this verse is talking about is an anointing—a supernatural power for wisdom and revelation of "*insight into mysteries and secrets* in the [deep and intimate] knowledge of Him" (Eph. 1:17, AMP, emphasis added). It is clear in Scripture that God has secrets, and He wants to reveal them to us:

> He who dwells in the *secret place of the Most High* shall abide under the shadow of the Almighty.
>
> —PSALM 91:1, EMPHASIS ADDED

> Then *I will give them heart to know Me*, that I am the LORD; and they shall be My people, and I will be their God, for they shall return to Me with their whole heart.
>
> —JEREMIAH 24:7, EMPHASIS ADDED

But *there is a God in heaven who reveals secrets*, and He has made known to King Nebuchadnezzar what will be in the latter days. Your dream, and the visions of your head upon your bed, were these.
—DANIEL 2:28, EMPHASIS ADDED

But as it is written: *"Eye has not seen, nor ear heard*, nor have entered into the heart of man the things which God has prepared for those who love Him." But God has revealed them to us through *His Spirit*. For the Spirit searches all things, yes, the deep things of God.
—1 CORINTHIANS 2:9–10, EMPHASIS ADDED

We need supernatural eyesight to see and understand the mysteries and secrets of God, but the wonderful news is that God wants us to know His secrets. The Bible says, "And you will seek Me and find Me, when you search for Me with all your heart" (Jer. 29:13). Why does God want us to know His secrets? The answer can be found in Deuteronomy 29:29: "The secret things belong to the LORD our God, but *those things which are revealed belong to us* and to our children forever" (emphasis added). The secrets of the Lord belong to Him until they are revealed; then they belong to us.

Before I accepted Christ as my Savior, salvation was a mystery to me. I didn't know that I needed to be born again. But on May 2, 1986, the mystery of salvation was revealed to me, and if I simply yielded to it, I would be saved. Many godly Christians die of sickness every day. They have received the revelation of salvation, but they have yet to understand the mystery of Isaiah 53:5, which says, "He was wounded for our transgressions, He was bruised for our iniquities; the chastisement for our peace was upon Him, *and by His stripes we are healed*" (emphasis added).

Once the mystery of the healing power of Christ's stripes is revealed, then we have access to His healing power. When you *see* it, you can *have* it. When the mystery is revealed, it rightfully belongs to you. It is your inheritance. It does the heir no good to have an inheritance he knows nothing about. Only when the heir sees and understands what is rightfully his can he take possession of it.

In Ephesians 1:17–19 Paul is praying by the Holy Spirit that God will give you insight into mysteries and secrets "in the [deep and intimate] knowledge of Him" (Eph. 1:17, AMP). This is because once you see the secrets, you have legal access to them for you are "joint heirs with Christ" (Rom. 8:17).

One of the jobs of the Holy Spirit is to show us the secrets of God. John 16:13–14 says, "When He, the Spirit of truth, has come, *He will guide you into all truth*; for He will not speak on His own authority, but whatever He hears He will speak; and He will tell you things to come. He will glorify Me, for *He will take of what is Mine and declare it to you*" (emphasis added).

God wants to open your spiritual eyes to see—the eyes of your heart, your understanding—"by having the eyes of your heart flooded with light, so that you can know and understand the hope to which He has called you" (Eph. 1:18, AMP).

Mankind has two sets of eyes. We have our natural eyes, and we have our spiritual eyes. We will see things with our spiritual eyes that our natural eyes will never see. It is the prayer of the Holy Spirit that the eyes of our heart be "flooded with light." We will discuss the reason for this at length in the next chapter, but suffice it to say that when we receive the light of the knowledge of Christ, we enter a new level of warfare that breaks the stronghold of insecurity and inferiority.

THE LIGHT OF JESUS

God commanded light to shine out of darkness. Second Corinthians 4:6 says He "has shone in our hearts to give the *light of the knowledge of the glory of God* in the face of Jesus

Christ" (emphasis added). It was at this point that the vision took hold of me. The light of the knowledge of the glory of God is revealed in the face of Jesus. I saw in an open vision the Word of God. The words of 2 Corinthians 4:6 were suspended in the air, and from within the words themselves I saw a visible bright, blue-white light.

It was the most beautiful light I had ever seen, and it represented the visible glory of God. I fell to my knees and cried out, "I see it! I see it!" Then God spoke to me and said, "Through My Word you will see Me."

The spirit of wisdom and revelation came upon me and opened my eyes to see the mystery of the gospel, "which is *Christ in you, the hope of glory*" (Col. 1:27, KJV, emphasis added). This event changed my life and forever changed the course of my ministry. It was the revelation of Christ that would change everything. As 1 John 3:2 says, when we see Him as He is, we will be changed.

16
EYES TO SEE

By having the eyes of your heart flooded with light, so that you can
know and understand the hope to which He has called you.
—EPHESIANS 1:18, AMP

A s WE DISCUSSED in the previous chapter, we have two sets of eyes because we live in two worlds. We live in a natural world, but we also live in a spirit world. With our natural eyes, we perceive visually the world around us. With our spiritual eyes—the eyes of our heart, our understanding— we see things that are beyond the natural realm.

God wants to flood the eyes of our heart with light—"the light of the knowledge of the glory of God in the face of Jesus Christ" (2 Cor. 4:6). When this happens, it moves us into a whole new dimension of spiritual warfare that breaks the hold of insecurity and inferiority off our lives.

Eve was deceived into eating the fruit because she lost sight. She lost sight of the revelation of God; therefore she lost sight of who she was. Our strength to defeat the enemy and close the door to insecurity and inferiority comes in our ability to see the light of the knowledge of Christ. The only reason we become subject to insecurity and inferiority is because we fail to see as God sees.

In his prayer in Ephesians 1:18, the apostle Paul went to the root of our battle with insecurity and inferiority and every other wile of the devil. Paul prayed that the eyes of our heart would be flooded with light so that we "can know and understand the hope to which He has called [us]" (AMP).

God gives us supernatural vision so we can know and understand the *hope* of our calling, the *hope* of our salvation, the *hope* of God's purpose for our life. We read in Colossians 1:27, "To them God willed to make known what are the riches of the glory of this mystery among the Gentiles: *which is Christ in you, the hope of glory*" (emphasis added). This is the root cause and solution to the problem. When we fail to see ourselves and others as God sees us, we become vulnerable to the spirits of insecurity and inferiority.

The prayer of the Holy Spirit through Paul points to the solution needed. We must have supernatural eyes to see Him for three distinct purposes. Understanding these divine purposes will give us the power to fulfill our God-given assignments individually and corporately.

THE HOPE OF OUR CALLING

The first of the purposes for Christ's coming revealed in Ephesians 1:18 is that we would *know and understand the hope of our calling*. This expresses itself in a couple of different ways. If you ask most Christians what their purpose is here on the earth, they won't be able to give you a very specific answer. They may recite some scriptures about evangelizing or showing forth the praises of God, but it is clear by their daily lives that these are only words and not revelation. You cannot truly understand your calling until you understand Jesus's calling.

Most Christians will tell you that the main reason Jesus came to the earth was to pay the price for our sins. I want to submit to you that He came for a much greater purpose, and that the work accomplished on the cross is much bigger than just forgiveness of sins.

Jesus in the Gospels and the Holy Spirit through the

Epistles make constant references to Christ's purpose for coming to earth:

> Just as the Son of Man did not come to be served, but to serve, and to give His life a ransom for many.
> —MATTHEW 20:28

> *I have come that they may have life*, and that they may have it more abundantly.
> —JOHN 10:10, EMPHASIS ADDED

> *And this is eternal life, that they may know You*, the only true God, and Jesus Christ whom You have sent. I have glorified You on the earth. *I have finished the work which You have given Me to do.*
> —JOHN 17:3–4, EMPHASIS ADDED

> *That they all may be one*, as You, Father, are in Me, and I in You; that they also may be one in Us, that the world may believe that You sent Me. *And the glory* which You gave Me I have given them, that they *may be one just as We are one*: I in them, and You in Me; *that they may be made perfect in one*, and that the world may know that You have sent Me, and have loved them as You have loved Me.
> —JOHN 17:21–23, EMPHASIS ADDED

And the grand-slam purpose for Christ's coming is found in 1 John 3:8: "*For this purpose* the Son of God was manifested, *that he might destroy the works of the devil*" (KJV, emphasis added). Jesus didn't just come to forgive us of our sins. He came to fully restore to us *all* that was lost in the garden—to reconcile us back to our original purpose, which can be found only in the revelation of God.

God created man after His own image and in His own

likeness (Gen. 1:27). When man sinned, he not only was kicked out of the Garden of Eden, but he also lost his connection to the glory of God. Man's purpose was not to just be a created being or to walk with God. God created mankind so He could eternally dwell in, and express Himself through, man.

God wanted to share all that He has and all that He is with someone, so He created man. When man sinned, it separated him from God and thwarted the plans of God. So God immediately put a strategy into place to not just forgive man but to restore him to God's original purpose, which was to have someone with whom He could share Himself.

This is why Christ came—to restore man to the place the Father always meant for him to have. He wanted to share His glory with us. This is why Christ came—to restore the glory:

> The mystery which has been hidden from ages and from generations, but now has been revealed *to His saints*. To them God willed to make known what are the riches of the glory of this mystery among the Gentiles: *which is Christ in you, the hope of glory.*
> —Colossians 1:26–27, emphasis added

> For in Him the whole fullness of Deity (the Godhead) continues to dwell in bodily form [giving complete expression of the divine nature]. *And you are in Him*, made full and having come to fullness of life [in Christ you too are filled with the Godhead—Father, Son, and Holy Spirit—and reach full *spiritual stature*].
> —Colossians 2:9–10, amp, emphasis added

We must come into a revelation of the fact that one of the reasons Christ came and died for us was to restore us to God's original purpose for creating us. We have been given the highest position of all the creatures in the universe. We have been predestined by God to be conformed into His image—to be like Him, "for whom He foreknew, He also predestined to be conformed to the image of His Son" (Rom. 8:29).

God designed us to be joined as one with Him for eternity. Ephesians 5:31–32 says, "'For this reason a man shall leave his father and mother and be joined to his wife, *and the two shall become one flesh.*' This is a great mystery, *but I speak concerning Christ and the church*" (emphasis added).

He has set us at the highest position possible. He has placed on us the highest value possible. This revelation, when the body of Christ truly gets it, will shatter all inferiority. Remember, inferiority is the feeling of being lower in position or stature. The revelation of the hope of your calling, which is to be one with Christ, destroys the lie of inferiority.

Knowing "the hope of your calling" will also affect you in your daily life. When you understand the purpose of Christ, the daily purpose of your life will also begin to come into focus. As long as we don't understand what we are called to here on the earth, we will live unfruitful, ineffective lives. The lack of clear purpose opens the door for the enemy. Proverbs 29:18 makes it clear that "where there is no *vision*, the people *perish*: but he that keepeth the law, happy is he" (kjv, emphasis added). The New King James Version states it this way: "Where there is no *revelation*, the people *cast off restraint*; but happy is he who keeps the law" (emphasis added).

When people lack clear vision, revelation, and purpose, they cast off restraint. Clear vision empowers us to be morally disciplined. The apostle John puts it this way: "But we know that when He is revealed, we shall be like Him, for we shall see Him as He is. And everyone who has this hope in Him purifies himself, just as He is pure" (1 John 3:2–3).

In the world today many motivational speakers teach that a person must have a clearly stated mission or purpose in order to accomplish anything great. These speakers have tapped into a characteristic that God placed in man. It is the driving force that clear purpose provides that empowers men to do more than what many people think is possible. This quality of human nature, when surrendered to the revelation of Christ, will empower us to excel in everything we set our hands to do. Through the power of Christ and His Word in us nothing shall be impossible. John 15:7 says, "If you abide in Me, and My words abide in you, you will ask what you desire, and it shall be done for you."

The Hope of Our Inheritance

Not only does God through the spirit of wisdom want us to understand the hope of our calling, but He also wants us to know *how rich is His glorious inheritance* in the saints (Eph. 1:18). In order to reverse the work of Satan in the garden and forever close the door to the enemy, God wants us to realize that we have been given all He has. God has not withheld anything He has from the church. He placed a value on us that could never be matched, and He gave us everything He has—which is more than our minds can comprehend.

The Bible says Jesus is the legal heir of *all* things:

> …has in these last days spoken to us by *His Son, whom He has appointed heir of all things*, through whom also He made the worlds; who being the brightness of His glory and the express image of His person, and upholding all things by the word of His power, when He had by Himself purged our sins, sat down at the right hand of the Majesty on high, having become so much better than the angels, as He has by inheritance obtained a more excellent name than they.
>
> —Hebrews 1:2–4, emphasis added

And when we accepted Christ's gift of salvation, we became joint heirs with Him. (See Romans 8:16–17.) God has not withheld anything from us: "He who did not spare His own Son, but delivered Him up for us all, how shall He not with Him also freely give us all things?" (Rom. 8:32).

Whatever we ask in Jesus's name God has said He will give it to us.

> If you abide in Me, and My words abide in you, you will ask what you desire, and it shall be done for *you. By this My Father is glorified*, that you bear much fruit; so you will be My disciples.
> —JOHN 15:7–8, EMPHASIS ADDED

> And in that day you will ask Me nothing. Most assuredly, I say to you, *whatever you ask the Father in My name He will give you.* Until now you have asked nothing in My name. *Ask, and you will receive*, that your joy may be full.
> —JOHN 16:23–24, EMPHASIS ADDED

Many Christians have quoted these verses over and over again for years, but the reality is that they still haven't truly seen them work. So they go on about their business quoting and praying and not really seeing any fruit. Step by step the enemy once again challenges the truthfulness of God by causing us to wonder, "Does the Word really work?" Although many Christians won't admit it, they don't truly believe that whatever they ask for in Jesus's name, God will do. They waver in their hearts. The Bible says those who doubt don't receive anything.

> But let him ask in faith, with no doubting, for he who doubts is like a wave of the sea driven and tossed by the wind. *For let not that man suppose that*

he will receive anything from the Lord; he is a double-minded man, unstable in all his ways.

—JAMES 1:6–8, EMPHASIS ADDED

Sowing seeds of doubt is one of Satan's great tricks. When we pray while wavering and doubting, we receive nothing, which reinforces our doubt, which leads to further unanswered prayers and a vicious cycle of defeat. The problem goes back to a lack of revelation—a failure to see with spiritual eyes that God has already given to us everything that belongs to Him. It is our legal inheritance because we are joint heirs with Him.

Let's look at faith for a moment. The word *faith* comes from the Greek word *pistis*, which means fidelity or loyalty to an authority.[1] Faith is not a feeling. It is a state of being. It is a loyalty to God and His Word. In the simplest terms, it is a willful choice to believe and obey God's Word, regardless of your circumstances.

We can only truly do this as we receive a deepening revelation of Jesus. When we see Him, we become like Him. We are changed into His image and nature. We take on His character. Then and only then can we truly pray in faith and see that whatever we ask shall be done for us in Jesus's name. When we begin to see and understand that God has given us all things and that we truly are joint heirs with Christ, then we will begin moving down the path of true freedom. These truths must become more than words. They must become alive on the inside of us.

UNLIMITED POWER

The third breakthrough the spirit of wisdom and revelation gives to us is victory over all insecurity. It will give us such confidence in Christ and His power that *nothing* will ever be able to shake us. Ephesians 1 reveals an amazing truth about the incredible power of God.

> And [so that you can know and understand] what
> is the immeasurable and unlimited and surpassing
> greatness of His power *in and for us* who believe,
> as demonstrated in the working of His mighty
> strength, which He exerted in Christ when He
> raised Him from the dead and seated Him at His
> [own] right hand in heavenly [places].
> —Ephesians 1:19–20, amp, emphasis added

The same power that raised Christ from the dead—the unlimited, supernatural power of God—is *in us* and is *for us*. The same power that said, "Let there be light," and there was light; the same power that upholds the universe; the same power that parted the Red Sea; the same power that sent fire down from heaven to consume Elijah's offering, delivered Daniel from the lions' den, and destroyed the armies facing Gideon—that same power is *in* us. (See Genesis 1:3; Colossians 1:17; Exodus 14:21; 1 Kings 18:38; Daniel 6:22; Judges 7:15.)

Ephesians 3:20 says God is able "to do exceedingly abundantly above all that we ask or think, *according to the power that works in us*" (emphasis added). And 2 Corinthians 4:7 tells us, "We have this treasure in earthen vessels, that the excellence of the power may be of God and not of us."

How often does the enemy use our circumstances to make us feel powerless? When we go through difficult circumstances, we often feel like there is nothing we can do. We feel out of control. This is the very purpose of terrorism—to make people feel so powerless over the violence that they simply surrender. The feeling of powerlessness is so unsettling that people will do just about anything to get a sense of power and security back, even if that means surrender.

Why did whole countries surrender to Germany during World War II? Because they were afraid they didn't have the power to defeat Hitler and his army. They were afraid that if they tried to stand up for themselves, they would suffer greater losses than if they simply backed down. So after being attacked, many countries handed control over to the Germans without a fight.[2]

This is also what happened to many Jews. At first the Germans began requiring the Jews to move into the slums. The Jews, for the most part, followed the orders. Even though living in these ghettos was a level of bondage, they figured it was better than dying. They saw the strength of the German army and felt they could not defeat them in battle.[3] Therefore they had only two choices: die or surrender. So many surrendered.

Step by step the German control deepened, and the freedoms of the Jews were stripped away layer by layer. Each step they faced the two choices: fight and possibly die, or surrender. Most continued down the path of surrender. We have seen this repeated time and again throughout history with many nations and peoples.

The Nazi oppression continued. The Germans took the Jews from the slums and started to place them in "labor camps," better know as concentration camps. The bondage deepened, the suffering increased, and the death they tried to avoid through surrender crept up upon them.

The same thing is happening in the spirit realm today. The enemy has been attacking Christians. He has been threatening us through insecurity and inferiority. He has convinced many Christians, including preachers, that as long as we are here on this earth, we can never conquer the flesh. We hear time and again that as long as we are in the flesh, we will sin. When we buy into this, we have already begun down the path of surrender. If we give Satan an inch, little by little he will deepen his control and increase our suffering.

When we believe we can't stop being slaves to sin, we believe the lie that the power of the cross is not sufficient. We believe that the power of sin is too great, and the best we can hope for is to avoid some sins. We become so convinced we can't win that we easily give up. We just accept certain "struggles" in our lives as part of who we are. In an attempt to spiritualize our situation, we even say that this area of sin is our "thorn in the flesh" (2 Cor. 12:7).

This mind-set allows the enemy to gain deeper control through fear and intimidation, until we find ourselves living a defeated life. We willingly follow Satan's commands because in our hearts we don't believe we have the power to defeat the enemy. The devil is a liar! The Bible is clear about the authority we have in Christ. Jesus said, "Behold, I give you the authority to trample on serpents and scorpions, and *over all the power of the enemy*, and nothing shall by any means hurt you" (Luke 10:19, emphasis added). And we are promised in Matthew that God has given us power to bind the works of the enemy:

> Assuredly, I say to you, whatever you bind on earth will be bound in heaven, and whatever you loose on earth will be loosed in heaven. Again I say to you that if two of you agree on earth concerning anything that they ask, it will be done for them by My Father in heaven. For where two or three are gathered together in My name, I am there in the midst of them.
>
> —MATTHEW 18:18–20

We have been give power and authority. We have the right to exercise the miracle-working power of God. Because we lack a revelation of the power that is in and for us who believe, we allow the enemy to not only keep us in the bondage of sin but also to prevent us from bringing to the world the resurrection power of Christ. We say things like, "I don't have the gift of healing or the power to work miracles. God has given that to a select few like Morris Cerullo or Benny Hinn." The devil is a liar. The Bible is clear that we are *all* to walk in the supernatural power of God. Jesus said:

> And these signs will [*not maybe, but will*] follow those who believe: In My name they *will cast out demons*; they *will speak with new tongues*; they *will take up serpents*; and if they drink anything deadly, it will by no means hurt them; they *will lay hands on the sick*, and they will recover.
>
> —MARK 16:17–18, EMPHASIS ADDED

The spirit of wisdom and revelation will give you access to the power to defeat the enemy and to show the world that Jesus is who He claims to be. Praise be to God! The fullness of Christ and His power has been given to us. He is in us. There is no power in hell or on earth that can overwhelm what is in us. We are totally secure because of the One who lives in us.

First John 4:4 assures us of this. It declares, "You are of God, little children, and have overcome them, because *He who is in you is greater than he who is in the world*" (emphasis added). And again we read in Isaiah 54:17, "'No weapon formed against you shall prosper, and every tongue which rises against you in judgment You shall condemn. This is the heritage of the servants of the LORD, and their righteousness is from Me,' says the LORD."

God wants to give to you the spirit of wisdom and revelation so you will know the hope of your calling, your inheritance, and the power that is in and for you. As the revelation of Christ continues to work in you, it will eradicate every open door the enemy has to plant insecurity and inferiority. Without those two roots all the other demon spirits have nothing to hold on to, and their power is easily broken.

17

WALK IN FREEDOM

*Draw near to God and He will draw near to you. Cleanse your
hands, you sinners; and purify your hearts, you double-minded.*
—JAMES 4:8

T HE REVELATION OF insecurity and inferiority will
continue to grow in your life. As God opens your eyes,
you will see the truth of God's Word work, and you will
see how these two demon spirits affect so much of what we do.
The power of the revelation of Christ to break these strongholds
cannot be underestimated. That is why the enemy fights so hard
in our lives and in our churches to keep the true depth of this
revelation from us.

Satan has done a masterful job of getting the church side-
tracked with programs and church-growth strategies that
appease the masses but truly do little to bring people to the
depths of revelation that will free them. This breakthrough is
not a superficial experience. You will not walk in complete victory simply by going to church on Sunday mornings, attending
an occasional Bible study, paying your tithes, and being a good
person.

We *all* need to go much deeper in the Spirit to a place found
only by those who are truly seeking the riches of God's glory.
The Bible makes it clear that when we search for Him, we will
find Him. Hebrews 11:6 says, "Without faith it is impossible to
please Him, for he who comes to God must believe that He is,
and that He is a rewarder of those who diligently seek Him."

129

And again, James 4:8 says, "Draw near to God and He will draw near to you. Cleanse your hands, you sinners; and purify your hearts, you double-minded."

God reveals His mysteries and secrets to those who are passionate and committed to pursuing holiness. We read in Matthew 5:8, "Blessed are the pure in heart, for they shall see God." And Hebrews 12:14 says, "Pursue peace with all people, and holiness, without which no one will see the Lord."

Sadly, much of the modern-day church is more interested in enjoying the worship service, sending their kids to a good children's program, and fellowshiping with their Christian friends than in pursuing a deep, surrendered, committed relationship with God. We have become comfortable in our lethargy and committed to our complacency.

The problem in the world today is not that there is too much sin or evil. The problem is that there is too little Jesus being revealed. Light dispels darkness, and the light of the revelation of Christ destroys the darkness of this world. This is the battle of our lives, the battle of our minds. Whose words will dominate and control the way we think? Whoever controls the mind of a man controls that man.

If the thoughts of insecurity and inferiority rule even part of your mind, then the enemy has a stronghold upon which he *will* launch further assaults. If the thoughts of Christ rule your mind, then you will be truly free in every area.

Take time to reread this book and meditate on the truths and scriptures presented here. Let the Holy Spirit release divine understanding inside of you so you can truly begin walking down the path of freedom. Satan has not changed his tactics since the beginning. He launches the same plan of attack today as he did in the Garden of Eden. When we identify and deal with these attacks of the enemy through the spirit of wisdom and revelation, the victories we shall walk in will be astounding. Christ will truly be formed in us, and the world will see the truth of John 8:36, that "if the Son makes you free, you shall be free indeed."

NOTES

CHAPTER 2
A SETUP IN THE GARDEN

1.   Webster's New World Dictionary (New York: Simon & Schuster, 1984), s.v. "insecurity."

2.   Ibid., s.v. "inferiority."

CHAPTER 6
MISPLACED IDENTITY

1.   James Thompson and Edgar Johnson, *An Introduction to Medieval Europe 300–1500* (New York: W. W. Norton and Company, 1937), 30, 36; Peter Brown, *The Cult of the Saints: Its Rise and Function in Latin Christianity* (Chicago: The University of Chicago Press, 1981), 5, 18, 27.

CHAPTER 9
THE KEYS TO SUCCESSFUL WARFARE

1.   Mira Kirschbaum, "Improve Your Outlook: Don't Be So Quick to Blame Your Exhaustion on Something Physical: It Could be Your Emotions," *Shape*, April 2004, http://findarticles.com/p/articles/mi_m0846/is_8_23/ai_114749396/ (accessed September 8, 2011).

CHAPTER 10
TRUE AND FALSE REPENTANCE

1.   Biblesoft's *New Exhaustive Strong's Numbers and Concordance with Expanded Greek-Hebrew Dictionary*, PC Study Bible 3, copyright © 1994 Biblesoft and International Bible Translators, Inc. s.v. *"metanoeo,"* NT:3340.

2.   Ibid., s.v. *"exousia,"* NT:1849.

CHAPTER 11
SATAN'S ENDGAME

1.   Biblesoft's *New Exhaustive Strong's Numbers and Concordance with Expanded Greek-Hebrew Dictionary*, PC Study Bible 3, s.v. *"exousia,"* NT:1849.

2.   *Nelson's Illustrated Bible Dictionary* (Nashville: Thomas Nelson Publishers, 1986), s.v. "hosanna."

CHAPTER 13
WALLS OF FEAR

1. Robert Jamieson, A. R. Fausset, and David Brown, *A Commentary, Critical and Explanatory, on the Old and New Testaments* (Oak Harbor, WA: Logos Research Systems Inc.).

2. Biblesoft's *New Exhaustive Strong's Numbers and Concordance with Expanded Greek-Hebrew Dictionary*, PC Study Bible 3, s.v. "*tharseo*," NT:2293.

CHAPTER 14
THE POWER OF AGAPE LOVE

1. Biblesoft's *New Exhaustive Strong's Numbers and Concordance with Expanded Greek-Hebrew Dictionary*, PC Study Bible 3, s.v. "*agapao*," NT:25.

2. Ibid., s.v. "*phileo*," NT:5368.

3. Ibid., s.v. "*martus*," NT:3144.

CHAPTER 15
THE SPIRIT OF WISDOM AND REVELATION

1. *Proof Producers*, Tape 1, Morris Cerullo, Morris Cerullo World Evangelism, 1983.

CHAPTER 16
EYES TO SEE

1. Biblesoft's *New Exhaustive Strong's Numbers and Concordance with Expanded Greek-Hebrew Dictionary*, PC Study Bible 3, s.v. "*pistis*," NT:4102

2. United States Holocaust Memorial Museum, "World War II in Europe," http://www.ushmm.org/wlc/en/article.php?ModuleId=10005137 (accessed September 12, 2011).

3. United States Holocaust Memorial Museum, "Ghettos," http://www.ushmm.org/wlc/en/article.php?ModuleId=10005059 (accessed September 12, 2011).